About the author

The Reverend Ron Dale entered the ministry after seven years in the electrical wholesale business and two years as a military dog handler in Libya. He has worked on a variety of Methodist circuits as pastor, superintendent and preacher, combining this with part-time teaching, industrial chaplaincy, broadcasting with the BBC regional network in Birmingham, Derby, Devon, Cornwall and the Channel Islands, prison chaplaincy and a considerable involvement with ecumenical work. He is married with two adult children.

Publisher's note

This book was originally designed to complement the Revised Common Lectionary. Where the Gospel readings for the Common Worship Lectionary differ, we have endeavoured to direct the user to the readings relevant to that Gospel reading, or to provide an alternative reading.

Contents

Foreword

I wrote the previous volume in this series, *Windows on Matthew*, during a three-month sabbatical that afforded me the time and space to research and plan it. When I was discussing the project with the publishers, it became clear that, if we were to do the first volume, two further volumes would be called for, one for St Mark's Gospel and one for St Luke's Gospel. This would complete the Gospel cycle used in the new Lectionary, the *Revised Common Lectionary*, soon to be adopted by all the mainstream churches worldwide.

While my first reaction was to say no, because on top of a busy circuit ministry three anthologies in three years seemed like an overload of work, I was gently persuaded and returned home to map out my time-table and set myself the necessary deadlines to achieve the publication dates.

As the months rolled by, I discovered that the age of miracles is not past! Both Mark and Luke have reached completion. Having received a great deal of positive feedback from readers of *Windows on Matthew*, my hope is that *Windows on Mark* will prove equally illuminating and stimulating. Like the Matthean volume, the stories, anecdotes and quotes in this book are offered for use not only by the preacher but also by the person in the pew, in whatever way helps to make the old, old story of the Gospel speak clearly today.

Finally, a note on the use of St John's Gospel in the Lectionary cycle, quoted from the Introduction of the *Revised Common Lectionary: The Consultation on Common Texts:*

> Fourth Gospel: Although it is not given a year of its own, the Gospel of John is used during the major seasons, the so-called 'festal' days of the year. Some see the inner outline of this Gospel as an attempt to provide a Christian understanding of the great festivals of the Jewish calendar; it is certainly not a sequential, chronological narration as much as it is a liturgical, theological exposition of the paschal mystery.

RON DALE: 1999

First Sunday of Advent

Mark 13:24-37

God comes

How do you think God would come to you?

In such a casual way we say, 'God comes'. How can we take for granted so bold a claim! Try to imagine for a moment the supreme Intelligence who dreamed a world and set the stars on their courses. To say such a God cares about humankind almost seems like a blubbering arrogance. And yet, this is our faith.

But the wisdom of the Bible was never very logical. People were always so sure that God stood on the rim of space and looked down at humanity with little more than scorn or pity or an occasional act of benevolence. They were so sure – until they looked into the face of a child in a manger and dared to say, 'God is with us'.

People were always so sure that God was like a king who enjoyed his power and dominated his subjects – until they looked into the face of a carpenter riding a donkey into a city and saw him make weak people strong.

People were always so sure that God would want them to deal cruelly with all who were different from his favoured worshippers. They were so sure – until they looked in the face of a man on a cross asking Father God to forgive his tormentors.

Remembering these things – how do you think God would come to you?

Ira E. Williams, Jun.
God in Unexpected Places

Come, Lord Jesus

Come, infant Jesus, come! It's been so long since anyone made us stop and think what all our callous schemes do to the babies of the world.

Come, boy Jesus, come! It's been so long since anyone noticed that the questions of a twelve-year-old might be important.

Come, carpenter Jesus, come! It's been so long since anybody dared to believe God might be standing at a workbench as surely as in church.

Come, teacher Jesus, come! It's been so long since most of

us dared to think we still have something to learn – we're too busy talking to listen.

Come, friend Jesus, come! It's been so long that we've used our friends for stepping-stones to success, we've forgotten how to care for one another.

Come, physician Jesus, come! It's been so long that our bitter words and spiteful deeds have split us apart, we need to be made whole again.

Come, crucified Jesus, come! It's been so long that we've excused our sins, we need someone who will make us see what hate and prejudice do when they have run full course.

Come, living Christ Spirit, come! Bring the powers of holy love to roll away the stone from the joyless tombs in which we've trapped ourselves.

And he said, 'Have I been with you so long, and yet you do not know me? . . . I am with you always!'

Ira E. Williams, Jun.
God in Unexpected Places

What is the significance today of Jesus' command to watch?

Many still, like the first readers, understand 'watch' as a call to expect a literal return of Jesus Christ, the Son of Man, in the immediate future. Some who hold to this literal interpretation erroneously identify specific current events with various troubles spoken of in Mark 13:5b-23 (already fulfilled at the time of the first readers) and say, 'Now is the time'. Others, taking seriously the warning that the time is unknown (Mark 13:32), still insist that he is coming literally (Mark 13:31) and that he is coming very soon (Mark 13:30). 'Generation' is sometimes interpreted to mean the life span of the entire human race, but hearers or readers are led to expect the return of Jesus in their own lifetime, just as the first hearers and readers did. This interpretation of 'watch' stresses the urgency of an immediate, future hope. It has always sustained oppressed people, like the Afro-American slaves who sang, 'My Lord, what a morning, when the stars begin to fall'.

A second option is to rationalise the future hope in terms that offer pragmatic guidance for the present. An example of this interpretation is seen in the story of an eclipse in colonial New England during which state legislators panicked and several moved to adjourn. But one of them said, 'Mr Speaker, if it is not the end of the world and we adjourn, we shall appear to be fools. If it is the end of the world, I should choose to be found doing my duty. I move you, sir, that candles be brought.' This understanding of 'watch' stresses the dimension of present responsibility.

A third option is to demythologise the language of Mark 13 and to understand the coming of the Son of Man as the realisation of the rule of God in one's own experience. This eschatological (final, definitive) encounter with Christ might come as the resolution of some period of severe trial, as a divine invasion accompanying the collapse of one's natural self-understanding, or at the end of one's life. It understands eschatology in terms of the quality of present existence, for it anticipates an encounter with the Son of Man in each one's Galilee (cf Mark 16:7).

On either the literal, the pragmatic, or the existential interpretation, the vision of the future in Mark 13 serves to strengthen discipleship in the present. It arms us against the wiles of deceivers (verses 5b-6, 21-23). It sustains us in whatever suffering or persecution we must endure (verses 8c, 13b, 20b). It motivates us to get on with preaching the Gospel to all nations (verse 10). It both ennobles and relativises the common round of daily life by making each moment subject to the invasion of the Son of Man, who comes to judge and to save . . .

Mark 13 speaks to those who expect too much and to those who expect too little. It is especially pertinent for those who have forgotten to expect anything at all.

Lamar Williamson, Jun.
Mark: Interpretation Bible Commentary

Second Sunday of Advent

Mark 1:1-8

Homing pigeon

Don't you move back now from the new age to the old age, from baptism and its freedom to circumcision and its bondage!

Why Jesus Never Wrote a Book is the title of a book Dr Sangster wrote over forty years ago.

In it he tells how in Germany in 1932 a lady found a pigeon on her doorstep. There was also a threatening note demanding money. Unless the lady put a large sum of money in the special containers strapped to the bird's legs, her house would be burned down. She informed the police, who chartered two aircraft, tied ribbons to the bird's neck, and told the pilots to follow.

When the pigeon landed, one pilot took a photograph of the house, and the other dropped a note to the police.

They dashed to the house, caught two brothers untying the ribbons and arrested them. But they said the bird wasn't from their loft, it was a stray. So the police did a test. They released the bird many times and every time it came back. Finally the two men broke down and confessed their guilt.

Evil is like that. It comes home.

When my own did, I wrote down all the bad things I'd said or done into an old notebook, asked God's forgiveness for every one, and burned the book. It was like a ten ton weight taken off my back, and I knew for myself the truth of St John's words: 'If we freely admit that we have sinned, we find God utterly reliable and straightforward. He forgives our sins and makes us thoroughly clean.'

Marvellous assurance that.

Though I can't speak for you, I freely admit that I need that forgiveness every day.

Ron Dale
Never on Sunday: Broadcast Talks

Dr William Sangster was a past president of the Methodist Church, a gifted scholar and preacher. He died in the 1960s.

A hymn to God the Father

Wilt Thou forgive that sin where I begun,
    which is my sin, though it were done before?
Wilt Thou forgive that sin, through which I run,
    and do run still: though still I do deplore?
When Thou hast done, Thou hast not done,
    for, I have more.

Wilt Thou forgive that sin by which I have won
    others to sin? And made my sin their door?
Wilt Thou forgive that sin which I did shun
    a year, or two: but wallowed in, a score?
When Thou hast done, Thou hast not done,
    for I have more.

I have a sin of fear, that when I have spun
    my last thread, I shall perish on the shore;
    swear by Thyself, that at my death Thy son
    shall shine as He shines now, and heretofore;
    and, having done that, Thou hast done,
    I fear no more.

John Donne

In Paul's letter to the Galatians, circumcision represents the old age. Circumcision, says Paul, is pre-Christian. Why? Because it discriminates and does not liberate. Circumcision is bad news, not good news. Why? Because it does not equalise but divides. It divides male from female. It divides Jew from Gentile. It is exclusive, not inclusive, the way baptism is. That's why Paul lashes out against those Jewish Christians who want to hang on to circumcision. Christ redeemed us from circumcision, and all the divisions it promoted, Paul proclaims. Don't you move back now from the new age to the old age, from baptism and its freedom to circumcision and its bondage!

In the old age the Jews had religious advantages over the Greeks. In the old age the free had social advantages over the slaves. In the old age, the men had religious and social advantages over the women. That situation is now at an end, says Paul. That advantage went out with baptism.

When you were baptised, you drowned to your old advantages. When you were baptised, you rose to the kind of life in which no one has advantage over another. When you were baptised, the whole business of privileged status went by the board. All racial, social and sexual distinctions were deprived of their advantage . . .

As these new Christians went down under water, as they drowned to their old, pagan way of life, as they drowned to the old age in which they once lived, all the divisions that marked their old way of life drowned along with them. All the twisted and perverted social relationships drowned along with them. At least they did so symbolically, for, as Frederick Buechner reminds us, the old Adam and the old Eve are mighty good swimmers. . . . Race, social class and sex: these were the Berlin Walls of the Jewish world. Poor you, if you were a Gentile. Poor you, if you were a slave. Poor you, if you were a woman.

John Timmer
Sermon called *Owning up to Baptism*

The chief actor in the historic mission of the Christian Church is the Holy Spirit. He is the director of the whole enterprise. The mission consists of the things that he is doing in the world. In a special way it consists of the light that he is focusing upon Jesus Christ.

This fact, so patent to Christians in the first century, is largely forgotten in our own. So we have lost our nerve and our sense of direction and have turned the divine initiative into human enterprise. 'It all depends on me' is an attitude that is bedevilling the practice and the theology of our mission in these days.

That is precisely what Jesus forbade at the start of it all. They must NOT go it alone. They must NOT think that the mission is their responsibility.

While he was in their company he told them not to leave Jerusalem. 'You must wait,' he said, 'for the promise made by my Father, about which you have heard me speak: John, as you know, baptised with water, but you will be baptised with the Holy Spirit, and within the next few days' (Acts 1:4-5). . . . By taking permanent hold of the waiting disciples as he had taken hold of Jesus, the Holy Spirit effected a kind of extension of the incarnation, bringing them into everything that could be available to them in Christ. This was their 'Christening' by which they were made to be as Christ in the world, his body filled with his very Spirit. Contrary to many sermons, the Holy Spirit was only incidentally given to empower them for their mission; the direct result of his coming was an outburst of praise to the Lord of whose presence in their midst they had suddenly been made aware. The polyglot crowd, overhearing and miraculously understanding, asked one another, 'What can this mean?' As Bonhoeffer puts it: 'The Spirit says through the Church the one word which everyone understands. It is a word that makes men responsible, even though the word is capable of mockery and misrepresentation, and that is the price of the visibility of the Church. This is the true sequence of mission: a surpassing awareness of the reality of Christ, corporately shared, expressing itself in thankfulness and wonder, causing the world to ask questions to which an answer must be given in a form that every hearer can understand . . .'

As one by one men and women have their eyes opened to see the overmastering reality of Christ and put their faith in him, they are baptised in the Holy Spirit and joined to the Spirit-filled society. For the Spirit's power, as well as his mission towards the whole world, operates always in the interactions of community rather than in the recesses of the individual soul. The Church, then, because it is possessed by the Spirit of the New Man, Jesus Christ, lives the life of the new mankind in the midst of the old world.

John V. Taylor
The Go-between God

Third Sunday of Advent

John 1:6-8, 19-28

Every interpretation of life carries intellectual difficulties. I can only set down my own word that Christ answers for me more questions than any other.

'Ain't it wonderful, Fynn?' she said, pointing to the dot. 'That might be the shadow of a shadow of a shadow of me or a bus or anything – or it might be you.'

I had a good look at myself. I didn't recognise myself but I got the point.

She unwound a dot to a straight line, from a line to a shape, from a shape to an object, from an object to a . . . Before she knew where she was, she was climbing like a monkey up the tree of higher and higher dimensions. An object, you see, might after all be the shadow of something more complex, and that something might be the shadow of something even more complex, and so on. The mind boggles at the thought. But there was really nothing to it, so I was told. Once you had managed to reduce everything to a dot, you couldn't reduce it any further. That was the end of the line, but as soon as you started to unwind things again, well, where did you stop? There was no reason why you shouldn't go on for ever. Except, of course, that there was one thing in this universe that was so complex that it couldn't become any more so. Even I guessed that one. None other than Mister God. Anna had reached the end of an infinite series of dimensions. At one end of the series was a 'dot', at the other end Mister God.

Feeding the ducks in the park the next day, I asked her how she had got on to the idea of shadows.

'In the Bible,' she announced.

'Where in the Bible?'

'Mister God said he would keep the Jews safe under his shadow.'

'Oh.'

'And then St Peter.'

'Wot about St Peter? Wot he do?'

'Made people better.'

'How'd he do that?'

'He put his shadow on ill people.'

'Oh! Yes. I should have known.'

'An' Old Nick.'

'How did he get in?'

'Wot's his name?'

'Satan.'

'Another one.'

'The Devil?'

'No. Another one.'

Finally I hit on Lucifer.

'Yes. Wot's it mean?'

'Light, I think.'

'How about Jesus?'

'Yeah – how about Jesus?'

'Wot's he say?'

'Lots of things, I suppose.'

'What did he call himself?'

'The Good Shepherd?'

'Something else.'

'Er – the Way?'

'Something else.'

'Oh, you mean the Light?'

'Yes. Old Nick and Jesus – both the light. You know what Jesus said, don't you? "I am the Light".' She stressed the word 'I'.

'What did he say it like that for?'

'So's you won't get muddled.'

'Two kinds of light – a pretend one and a real one. Lucifer and Mister God.'

Fynn
Mister God this is Anna

The story of Anna told by Fynn took place over 50 years ago. Whilst roaming the London dockland area one foggy night he picked up from the gutter a dirty, bruised and injured little girl and took her home to his mum. Later on, Anna's main occupation in life was being a personal friend and helper of Mister God. She knew the purpose of being and the meaning of love. At six years she was a theologian, mathematician, philosopher, poet and gardener. At seven she died after a terrible accident, with a grin on her beautiful face, saying: 'I bet Mister God lets me get into heaven for this.' (Quote from flyleaf.)

If Christ is not the light of the world – of a world that has teased the philosophers since ever man reflected on the mystery of being, of suffering, of tragic conflict, of death – then to whom must we turn?

Through hundreds of years before the birth of Christianity, the Greeks had pondered the meaning of life and reality. A galaxy of thinkers, unrivalled before or since, had put every question the human mind is capable of putting, and received, maybe, the only answers the unaided mind of man will ever get to these problems. A great student of the subject says that at the end of this incomparable period the Greek lost his nerve. When he reviewed his gains, it was all so little to satisfy his heart, to fortify and support him in his pilgrimage through the shadows of our mortal life, that he fled to the mystery religions as an emotional exit. Then there was the cry of a child in a manger crib, a man working in a carpenter's shop, a voice like music heard over quiet waters at eventide, an awesome energy beyond the violence of the winds, more reasonable than the reasonings of men, older than primitive frenzy, and fresher than the dawn, at once new and familiar; and men lifted up their heads as though redemption drew nigh. In the eyes of this man they found the home of all their dreams. Enshrined in flesh and blood, in amazing actuality, they saw all they had ever wanted to be, and in the logic of life, of this man's life, the answer to their questions.

Strange paradox, this man had to be silenced before he was heard, killed before he could live in the hearts of men, and by submissions that proved more powerful than man's rebellions he stood Lord of life, and in his hands the seven stars. Through the generations of two thousand years humanity has drawn from him the deepest belief in life, in its meanings and possibilities, and faced death with eyes unafraid. His Gospel has furnished the mind with spacious imagery, and filled the heart with the poetry of the grace of God, has compelled men to uttermost sacrifice, educated the heart in the courtesies born of humility, put the mirth of God into the gloomy spirit, overcome every despairing philosophy, and provided the retort of the soul to enfeebling doubt. If that Gospel is passing, if that One is now discredited, then let us know there will be a darkness where we badly want a light, and a silence where we badly want a voice. If we must turn from him, then we turn from the most beautiful and the most satisfying thoughts of God, of life and death, that man has ever entertained. . . .

Every interpretation of life carries intellectual difficulties. I can only set down my own word that Christ answers for me more questions than any other. And as far as the problems of my life are concerned, and they are the problems that matter most to me, he satisfies them all. With these assurances I open my heart generously to him, a heart that longs for all he offers and promises, and in devotion of love I go my pilgrim way with an irrepressible song. Such unreserved faith has given the Church its most glorious and fruitful days, and the men and women who have so accepted him live, for me, the most enviable life. With these arguments I turn and fall at his feet. Then the light of his countenance and the touch of his hand are the final proof that I am where I ought to be, and where the world must be if it is to be saved.

A. E. Whitham
The Discipline and Culture of the Spiritual Life

A. E. Whitham was a Methodist circuit minister, deeply committed and intensely spiritual. His daughter wrote of him in the introduction of the above book: 'He was truly a master in the art of living, and it was exhilarating to see him give himself fully and vigorously to that art. His poise was remarkable: his catholicity of mind, his genius for friendship, his patience in his dealings with folk who tried him sorely, his unforgettable humour . . . Methodism never had a more loyal son than he.'

Fourth Sunday of Advent

Luke 1:26-38

We are asked to carry the embryonic Christ in our hearts and to prepare for his coming again.

Advent used to be known as 'The Lent of St Martin' because it was a time for reflection upon judgement and the last days. It now offers the opportunity to start thinking about what the coming of Christ meant originally, and about what it means nowadays – when 'the depth of the human capacity for destructive evil is an aspect of reality which a twentieth-century man is unlikely to take lightly' (from an Advent order of service at St John's College, Cambridge). As well as being a season for feeding the hope of deliverance from evil, Advent is the time for the physical preparation for a modern Christmas.

Advent has been observed since the sixth century as a reminder to men that they must make themselves fit for Christ's arrival. It is also the occasion for singing the first carols. Some of them, including the best, are so old that they go back to the time when a carol was a dance in a ring, accompanied by a song, but quite unconnected with the church. An example is one, more than 600 years old and known to Chaucer, that has kept its dance tune:

Gabriel to Mary came,
a gentle message bare he;
deep in awe the Maiden bowed
to hear him say 'Hail Mary'.
There heaven and earth received his call,
'Hail, hail thou queen of virgins all;
thou, yet undefiled
shalt bear a child
of sovereign grace,
to comfort all mankind;
thou shalt bear him, Lord and God of all,
to save our human race'.

The complete translation from the medieval Latin, with the tune, is no. 1 in the *Penguin Book of Christmas Carols*.

Denys Thompson
Readings

'Will you carry me?'

Not long ago at a Catholic worker infant house, a shelter for battered and abused children, a small boy of about five was to be placed in a foster home. The woman who runs the house was walking him out to the car to meet his new foster parents when the boy, who had grown to feel very secure in his time at the shelter, asked her, 'Will you carry me?' The woman reached down to reassure him and said she thought he was getting a little too big to be carried. The boy responded by saying, 'I mean in your heart'. The woman was surprised that the small child spoke so figuratively and told him that she certainly would. As he got nearer the car he said, 'Will you remember to kiss me good night?' This time she knew he was not speaking literally and so she said she would; she would remember him each night, and she would carry him in her heart.

This story illustrates what is being asked of us in the pregnant time of Advent. Much is being asked of us: We are asked to carry the embryonic Christ in our hearts and to prepare for his coming again. We are asked to make room for him, to prepare a home so he will not always be consigned to the stable. And we are asked to comprehend that strong and mystical commingling in which we know ourselves and others to be a part of a divine and eternal life, the Body of Christ.

Penelope Duckworth
Teaching Sermons on the Incarnation

Christmas Day – First Proper

Luke 2:1-14 (15-20)

A fool sees not the same tree as a wise man sees.

The shepherd's carol

We stood on the hills, Lady,
    our day's work done,
    watching the frosted meadows
    that winter had won.

The evening was calm, Lady,
    the air so still,
    silence more lovely than music
    folded the hill.

There was a star, Lady,
    shone in the night,
    larger than Venus it was
    and bright, so bright.

Oh, a voice from the sky, Lady,
    it seemed to us then
    telling of God being born
    in the world of men.

And so we have come, Lady,
    our day's work done,
    our love, our hopes, ourselves
    we give to your Son.

Anonymous

Blake among angels

For the young child saw visions, even as he walked among the ditches and the brick kilns of the countryside around London. His mid-Victorian biographer tells the story best, or, at least, more plausibly: 'On Peckham Rye (by Dulwich Hill) it is, as he will in after years relate, that while quite a child, of eight or ten perhaps, he has his "first vision". Sauntering along, the boy looks up and sees a tree filled with angels, bright angelic wings bespangling every bough like stars. Returned home he relates the incident, and only through his mother's intercession escapes a thrashing from his honest father, for telling a lie. Another time, one summer morn, he sees the haymakers at work, and amid them angelic figures walking.' The vision of Peckham Rye may not, however, have been his first; his wife once reminded him of an earlier apparition. 'You know, dear, the first time you saw God was when you were four years old. And he put his head to the window and set you screaming.' And then again, 'even when a child his mother beat him for running in and saying that he saw the prophet Ezekiel under a tree in the fields'. The story of the father's threat to beat the child for seeing a tree filled with angels may be the source of a note made by a close friend after Blake's death: 'belief in his inspiration reprov'd by his father for asserting it.'

These visions were indeed his inspiration and, as Blake declared in one of his *Proverbs of Hell*, a fool sees not the same tree as a wise man sees. What Blake saw was not the crepuscular and dirty city of the historian's imagination, but a city filled with angels and prophets. He saw a biblical city.

Peter Ackroyd
Blake

When Christ was born

When Christ was born –
    wise men came from the East looking for a king
    and bringing costly treasures to gain favour from one
    who would sit on an earthly throne.
They found instead a peasant woman hovering over
    a baby wrapped in rags, and were moved to share
    their wealth with the homeless and shivering family.

When Christ was born –
    the zealots of the Jewish underground were looking
    for a leader with courage enough to drive the
    Roman army from their land.
They found instead a man who made them put
    away their swords and face the wrath of their enemies
    with no weapons but divine love and goodwill.

When Christ was born –
    the Pharisees were looking for a Messiah who
    would congratulate them for being such religious men.
They found instead a man whose look pierced the
    veneer of their bigotry and laid bare their empty souls.

When Christ was born –
    the beggars in Jerusalem were looking for a comrade
    who would sympathise with their resentment and
    help them soak the filthy rich.
They found instead a carpenter who made them
    stand on their feet with dignity and pride as they
    joined him in the tasks he had for them to do.

When Christ was born –
    the good people of Jerusalem were looking for a
    comforter to assure them that the sick and the poor
    at their gates had pretty well gotten what they deserved.
They found instead a physician who taught them
    to heal the sick and have compassion for the poor.

When Christ was born –
    he denied men what they asked for, and gave them
    what they needed. If that happens to you, don't become
    bitter – accept it thankfully.

Ira E. Williams, Jun.
God in Unexpected Places

J. B. Priestley's *Lost Empires* is set in 1913-14, just before the onset of the First World War. It is the story of young Richard Herncastle helping his uncle, an illusionist, play the now vanished music halls, the 'Lost Empires' of the title. Richard is the one who looks after all the props at each music hall on their tour and also takes the band call at the beginning of each week. They are soon to play in Nottingham and are making arrangements about where they shall stay for the duration of their visit.

On Saturday I told him [his uncle] and Cissie [his uncle's assistant] that I wouldn't be sharing their digs in Nottingham because I'd already arranged to stay with some people I knew there. He didn't care, but Cissie was disappointed. 'Oh Dick, I did hope we'd all be together for Christmas.'

'Don't start that girl,' Uncle Nick told her. 'I hate Christmas.'

'Nick, you don't.'

'I do. It's all so stupid.'

'But what about the kiddies?'

'What about the kiddies?' It was brutal mimicry. 'Well, what about 'em? They like Christmas because they get things given. They'd like any other time when they got things given. Middle of April – end of October – any time. The rest of us are just diddled by the shopkeepers, who raise their prices because they're so full of the Christmas spirit of good-will and peace to all men. I had a Christmas card today – all about old friendship and loving thoughts by the fireside – from the biggest rogue of an agent I've ever had to deal with. No, don't talk to me about Christmas, girl. I'll endure it, but I'm damned if I'll enjoy it. I earn a living by deceiving other people, but I don't have to deceive myself.'

J. B. Priestley
Lost Empires

Christmas Day – Second Proper

Luke 2:(1-7) 8-20

To enter the actual place where Christ was born every pilgrim has to bend low in order to pass through the tiny door.

Over the last twenty years or so I have been privileged to conduct Christian pilgrims around the Holy Land, visiting many of the well known places and shrines as and when the security situation allowed. So we would spend some time in and around Jerusalem before moving on to the lovely region of Galilee.

One day we were in the Church of the Nativity in Bethlehem, first built by the Empress Helena in AD 325, noting as we toured the building the original mosaic floor and some of the original frescos.

To enter the actual place where Christ was born every pilgrim has to bend low in order to pass through the tiny door, (a parable in itself, for all of us must stoop when entering into the presence of divinity). Once in the cave, the eyes of any pilgrim are drawn naturally to a solid silver star set in the floor, marking the spot where tradition has it that the Christ was born. Around the star are usually many pilgrims kneeling and pressing their eyes, lips and forehead on to the star as an act of piety and also in order to carry away a blessing.

On every occasion I have been with a group of pilgrims I ask someone to read the Christmas story, and after a prayer from me we quietly sing *Away in a manger, no crib for a bed*, and then I leave and let people have some private space and devotion before moving on, if possible, to the Herodian, King Herod's summer palace built on a dominant hillside just outside Bethlehem.

On one occasion I was walking back to the coach with a lady member of my group and noticed that she was emotionally distressed. Tears were rolling down her cheeks and from time to time she brushed them away with her fingers. I took her on one side and asked if she was fit to move on and she affirmed she was. After composing herself she told me the reason for her tears, saying some words that I shall always remember: 'To think that the Son of God should come to such a place as this for a mere nobody like me.' In her own eyes she was unworthy and a nobody, but I remembered and pondered what Mary said to her cousin Elizabeth after she had greeted her by saying: 'What an honour it is to have the mother of my Lord come to see me!' Mary responds with what we now call the *Magnificat*: 'My soul magnifies the Lord, and my spirit rejoices in God my Saviour. FOR HE HAS DEIGNED TO NOTICE ME, his humble servant. . . .'

Long afterwards the sheer wonder of those words hit me. 'He has deigned to notice me.' All of us, from whatever background or culture, is 'noticed' by God and therefore given value, meaning, direction and purpose within his amazing love revealed to the lady in Bethlehem that day and to all humankind.

Ron Dale

My predecessor, both as Chaplain of Trinity College, Cambridge, and as Vicar of St George's, Camberwell, the Trinity College Mission in South London, Geoffrey Beaumont, left Camberwell to become a monk. He joined the Community of the Resurrection; and they soon sent him off as a novice on something he hated: a beach mission on the sands at Felixstowe. He couldn't bear it, because people on holiday were 'got at' by a preacher. And there were lots of callow students to help the preacher – or that was the theory.

Geoffrey had only to stand around in the crowd in his cassock – after he'd gathered the crowd for the preacher from their deckchairs. He did, until he saw a notice: 'Bathing Costumes for Hire'. That did it. He slipped quietly away and hired one – a 1950s model; black, with shoulder straps; got into it, and rejoined the crowd. A few minutes later one of the students, not now recognising him without his cassock and his glasses, pursued him. 'Have you been saved?' tenderly she enquired. 'Saved?' he said, 'I haven't been in yet!'

There is a theological point to that story.

IN-CARNATION. Christmas and Epiphany are not in the end about candlelight, cribs, kings and incense in a sanctuary. They are about God in his world: inside the various situations which are most pressing. And we have to be immersed in those situations before we can work out what the Gospel has to say to them: what 'salvation' might mean.

Eric James
Judge Not: A Selection of Sermons

Sunday, 26 December 1742

From those words, 'Sing we merrily unto God our strength; make a cheerful noise unto the God of Jacob', I took occasion to show the usual way of keeping these days holy, in honour of the birth of our Lord; namely, by an extraordinary degree of gluttony and drunkenness; by heathen, and worse that heathen diversions (with their constant attendants, passion and strife, cursing, swearing and blasphemy); and by dancing and card playing, equally conducive to the glory of God. I then described the right way of keeping a day holy to the Lord – by thanksgiving; by hearing, reading and meditating on His word, and by talking of all His wondrous works.

The Journal of John Wesley, Vol. 3

They knelt at the manger

It wasn't an easy thing to do – what Mary did:
Hearing her friends whisper that she had to get married . . .
Making the long ride to Bethlehem on the back of a clumsy
    donkey . . .
Birthing her firstborn in a cowshed to be laid on the straw.
But she did it – and thanked God for the privilege.

It wasn't an easy thing to do – what Joseph did:
Believing in the innocence of the pregnant girl he was engaged
    to marry . . .
Accepting the abuse from short-tempered innkeepers in the
    little town . . .
Risking his life to take Mary and the baby to Egypt in the face
    of Herod's anger.
But he did it – and thanked God for the privilege.

It wasn't an easy thing to do – what the Wise Men did:
Crossing the desert to Bethlehem with no guide but a star
and a prayer of faith . . .
Giving their costliest possessions with no hope of receiving
in return . . .
Accepting the disfavour of a hotheaded king rather than betray
an innocent family.
But they did it – and thanked God for the privilege.

It wasn't an easy thing to do – what you did:
Giving an afternoon each week to call at the nursing home . . .
Praying for that man who did you wrong, in the presence of
your children . . .
Taking those Cuban kids into your home while their mother
was in hospital.
But you did it – and thanked God for the privilege.

In a way, YOU knelt at the manger, too!

Ira E. Williams, Jun.
God in Unexpected Places

Christmas Day – Third Proper

John 1:1-14

Back to basics: Revelation

Most of the truth which really matters comes to us not in abstract propositions but through the agency of personal encounter.

In this series we are getting back to basics and I want to talk to you this morning about revelation. This is probably the key problem of religion: how does God communicate with us? Some religions say – through the natural world, in the spirits that inhabit rocks and rivers and mountains. Others claim that an infallible book dropped from Heaven into the lap of their founder. Astrologers read the truth sketched out in the conformation of heavenly bodies, and there are those who say God speaks through the spirits of the dead. The prologue to John's Gospel says God communicates with us by the Word, the creative power of God, becoming flesh – divine truth invading a human personality.

Isn't it a fact that most of the truth which really matters comes to us not in abstract propositions but through the agency of personal encounter? An orphan will get precious little comfort from a manual of child care; he or she needs a mother. A medical dictionary is no cure for the seriously ill. They need the healing touch of a doctor or nurse. The lonely may get some comfort and companionship from their television set or radio but in the end they need a friend. And no doctrine of salvation can release someone imprisoned in a self-made hell. They need a saviour. Truth personalised – the Word become flesh.

Thus we address some of the most tantalising questions that tease the human mind. What is God like? How can we know, for who and what he is in himself is beyond the range of the senses. But the nearest we'll come to an answer is embodied in Jesus through whom millions have caught a vision of God's love in action, God's will being done on earth as it is in heaven. Does God care? Behold Jesus, ministering to heal a divided world, save a doomed world and dying to spell out the truth in blood. You ask: how can I reach God? You can't but he has reached you – put himself within range of your outstretched hand by raising Jesus from the dead and transforming him from a sacred memory into a living presence. And if you think that extravagant language, then there are millions willing to echo it and risk the sneers of the detractors and the disbelief of cynics by declaring that they know he lives because they've met him.

Philosophies are to be argued about; theologies to be expounded; ideas to be played around with, but the truth incarnate in personality demands a response. The Word became flesh to speak to us in a language we can understand.

So, one reason the Word became flesh was so that God could communicate with us in a language we can understand.

A second reason was this: the Word became flesh to weld God and his world together.

Word and flesh; God and the world. You cannot have one without the other. You cannot choose God and write off the world as irrelevant as some pietists want to do. Nor will you be able to remake the world without taking account of God, as many idealists struggle to do. If you want one, you must have the other. God without the world is an enigmatic abstraction; the world without God is a terrifying fiction.

Who, then, does this world belong to? Some misguided Christians say, 'To the Devil. Keep well clear of it.' Others would claim from their reading of history that the world belongs to whoever is strong enough to dominate it – so accept the inevitable. The New Testament says the world belongs to God so go in there and claim it for him. This is why a lot of people miss the point when they complain about what they call the Church's interference in politics. They don't understand or maybe we haven't made it clear enough, that the path to holiness leads us through the places where the action is the bloodiest, the compromises most degrading and the conditions most appalling. Because the Word has become flesh, it is in the places where flesh is tortured and starved and imprisoned that we shall especially find Christ.

If you were to ask me how I think God has revealed himself to me in a not uneventful life, I would answer something like this. Where have I seen the purity of God? Most clearly reflected in the face of one of Christ's disciples, a nun struggling against impossible odds to bring a touch of dignity and wholesomeness to the squalor of a teeming shanty town – an earthly parable of that tremendous truth in this prologue to John's Gospel that there is a Light which no darkness can extinguish. When have I known the peace of God? Not in the cloistered quiet of some retreat house, for I am one of those hyperactive Christians who, when asked to be still for any length of time and contemplate the ineffable being of God, tend to nod off. I've encountered the peace of God when in concert with others in several places in the world torn by violence, I've tried, however pathetically, to do some deed of human reconciliation. And the most moving evidence of

God's justice I've encountered was behind barbed wire where prisoners of conscience have refused to bow the knee to Baal.

Occasionally, like Moses, like most of us, I'm tempted to beg God for a minor miracle – a flashing vision or an unearthly voice to lift my flagging spirits as I trudge through the wilderness. And God tells me just what he told Moses – 'You shall not see my face but I will show you my back.' I too have seen God's back as I've watched streams of refugees being turned away from some African frontier post. And as they slouched away into oblivion, I realised that there, naked and scarred, was the sight of God's back.

It is commonly said that much of what goes on in our churches is irrelevant. To the extent that it is true, the reason is that the Church ceases to be relevant when the Word does not become flesh in it – it's transformed into majestic stone and glorious music and splendid architecture, but it does not become flesh. And if our prayers sometimes echo hollowly around the lofty vaults of our splendid churches, it's because our words remain words, they do not become flesh.

The Word became flesh to symbolise the dependence of God. Christianity shares many truths with other religions. One truth is unique to it. Whilst some religions make great play of human dependence on God, Christianity dares to speak of God's dependence on humanity. The Word, almighty power, irresistible force, becomes human flesh, frail and vulnerable to whatever is stronger than itself. Therefore, in becoming flesh, God put himself at our mercy, entrusting himself into our hands.

Wasn't that historically true? Didn't Jesus need a human womb in which to be born; a human breast at which to suck; a father to carry him into Egypt away from Herod's wrath; a group of friends to support and sometimes betray him; a conscript to carry his cross? It was true in the days of his flesh; it is true today. Does he not need human hands to wield the instruments through which he heals; a human voice to bring comfort to the distressed; human eyes to look in compassion on the lonely; a human presence to stand beside the outcast; human brain power to help make deserts fertile and feed the hungry; human political skills dedicated to creating a more just and humane social order?

The Word made flesh is a stupendous demonstration of faith. Not of our faith in God – that flickers and fades, waxes and wanes – but of God's faith in us, entrusting himself and the fate of his Kingdom into our shaky treacherous hands. In a sense all this is dramatised by what will happen in every mass or Eucharist celebrated throughout the Church. Believers will come to the altar or communion table and hold out their hands for the bread – and the priest or minister will use some such phrase as 'Body of our Lord Jesus Christ' – and it is as though Christ himself were being entrusted into our care to do with as we please.

You might call that God's supreme gamble, a cosmic wager, God taking a chance that we won't let him down. Just as the Word had to become flesh in the time of Pontius Pilate so that the world *might* be saved, it's only as the Word becomes flesh in us that the world will know that it is saved. Another way of putting that is to say that this is God's world but it will be what we make of it.

Rev. Colin Morris
Extract from a sermon on Anglia Television: Lent 1997

First Sunday of Christmas

Luke 2:22-40 (RCL)

The Mystery of Love . . . is always greater than the preacher's words or vision: it is greater than this world.

So it's not only tender shepherds who reveal the Mystery of Love. The prophets do so as well. And prophecy and preaching are near neighbours. (Perhaps the greatest preacher of our time has been Martin Luther King, whose sermons were published under the title *Strength to Love*.) But, you will remember, Martin Luther King was assassinated for what he preached – because he had the strength to say that the Mystery of Love and the cause of negro civil rights are inseparable.

Yet Martin Luther King's last sermon said something about the Mystery of Love: that it is always greater than the preacher's words or vision: it is greater than this world. He said – significantly, as I say, in his last sermon, just before he was assassinated:

'I don't know what will happen now.
We've got some difficult days ahead.
But it doesn't matter to me now.
Because I've been to the mountain top, I won't mind.
Like anybody else, I would like to live a long life.
Longevity has its place.
But I'm not concerned about that now.
I just want to do God's will.
And he's allowed me to go up to the mountain top.
And I've looked over, and I've seen the Promised Land.
So, I'm happy tonight. I'm not worried about anything.
I'm not fearing any man.
Mine eyes have seen the glory of the coming of the Lord . . .'

He had seen the Mystery of Love, and was interpreting it in terms of the realities of his surrounding world and society.

What a preacher has to do, I believe, is to point toward a Mystery, not to teach a system of thought and then demonstrate that nothing can disturb it . . . to point, again and again, in this way and that, to the Mystery of God's love at the very heart of the universe.

Eric James
Judge Not: A Selection of Sermons

That baffling cube

When the Rubic Cube came out I borrowed one and had many attempts to get all the coloured sides to match. I couldn't even get one side right.

I've known some fathers stay up into the small hours trying to master the Cube; children who have almost done it, and even marriages put under stress because husbands have been so hooked on it that they've ignored their wives. I only know one boy who can do the Cube, and it only takes him five minutes. I watch him very carefully, but I never seem to manage it. I must be really thick . . .

So it gives me a great sense of relief when I meet other parents who can't do the Cube. And I laughed long and loud at a photograph in the *Express and Echo* recently of a little girl dressed up as a Rubic Cube. She had just won a local fancy dress competition. The caption read: 'My mummy can't fathom me out.' Words I think that apply not only to the Cube but also, as time goes by, to the girl. For whilst I can imagine Mum saying to her daughter on occasions, 'I can read you like a book,' I can also imagine her saying, after a few years, 'Will I ever really know and understand you?'

Could it be that the only person who really knows us is God himself? Could it be that we only really know ourselves in his love?

Ron Dale
Never on Sunday: Broadcast Talks

Child of mine

Towards the end of May this year we spent a week's 'Pilgrimage Holiday' in the Belgian city of Bruges, a holiday arranged by Alan Heslop, the Warden of Morley retreat house, near Derby.

Bruges is sometimes called 'the Venice of the North' and a brief glance at its canals, gabled houses and cobbled alleys shows how apt that title is.

Three lofty buildings dominate the city's skyline: the Belfry in the Market Square with its tuneful carillon; St Saviour's Cathedral (Bruges' oldest parish church, dating from the twelfth century); and the Church of Our Lady. This church, with its spire just ten metres shorter than Salisbury Cathedral's, houses many fine works of art. Amongst them is Michelangelo's

Virgin Mary with the infant Jesus (1501). It is, I understand, one of the very few Michelangelo statues outside Italy.

What a masterpiece it is! It is an altarpiece and cannot be much more than four feet or so high. But, though relatively small scale, this sculpture is remarkable both for its detail (the folds in Mary's dress, for instance, and the tender interlocking of the mother's hand with her child's) and for the mood it projects. There is composure, yet preoccupation, less the pleasure of the mother-child relationship than the anticipation of sorrow yet to come. Already at Nazareth there is the painful awareness of Calvary ahead – suffering which old Simeon's blessing has prepared for.

At Christmas, if we have any time at all (and Christmas has been defined as the Xmas Mad Annual Scramble) we might call Bethlehem to mind and Mary with her child. All was not sweetness and light for them. Mary's circumstances and her future must have perplexed her. Where were events leading? Inexorably towards misunderstanding, loneliness, rejection, crucifixion. Beyond the angels of the Christmas story lies the angel of Gethsemane, strengthening the Son of God as he grapples with the cup of suffering.

For many of us in the coming year storm clouds will gather and some of the issues which confronted Mary we ourselves shall confront. It is then that the Christian faith, if not relevant to us before, may become powerfully relevant. Authentic Christianity does not promise immunity from suffering but a way of coping with it . . .

If we cannot get *round* suffering, we may find help to live *through* it. We may even achieve something of that quality so evident on the face of Michelangelo's Virgin Mary at Bruges – composure.

Child of mine, the Virgin sings,
    child of mine, yet King of kings,
    promised us by Gabriel,
    Jesus Christ, Emmanuel.

Child of mine – how can this be?
Child of mine – what mystery!
But things are as God has planned,
    all are safe within his hand.

Child of mine and gift from heaven;
    child of mine that God has given,
    firstborn son and precious boy,
    born to sorrow, born to joy.

Child of mine, soon sorrow's dart,
   child of mine, shall pierce my heart;
   but great joy is rising there,
   joy for all the world to share.

Child of mine among us now,
   Jesus Christ, come show us how
   love has come to drive out fear:
   all are blessed, for God is here!

Rev. David Mowbray
Child of Mine: A meditation for Christmas

First Sunday of Christmas

Luke 2:15-21 (CWL)

It is a lovely thought that the shepherds who looked after the Temple lambs were the first to see the Lamb of God who takes away the sin of the world.

It is a wonderful thing that the story should tell that the first announcement of God came to some shepherds. Shepherds were despised by the orthodox good people of the day. They were quite unable to keep the details of the ceremonial law; they could not observe all the meticulous hand-washings and rules and regulations. Their flocks made far too constant demands on them; and so the orthodox looked down on them. It was to simple men of the fields that God's first message came.

But these in all likelihood were very special shepherds. We have already seen how, in the Temple, morning and evening, an unblemished lamb was offered as a sacrifice to God. To see that the supply of perfect peace offerings was always available, the Temple authorities had their own private sheep flocks; and we know that these flocks were pastured near Bethlehem. It is most likely that these shepherds were in charge of the flocks from which the Temple offerings were chosen. It is a lovely thought that the shepherds who looked after the Temple lambs were the first to see the Lamb of God who takes away the sin of the world.

When a boy was born, the local musicians congregated at the house to greet him with simple music. Jesus was born in a stable at Bethlehem and therefore that ceremony could not be carried out. It is a lovely thought that the minstrelsy of heaven took the place of the minstrelsy of earth, and angels sang the song for Jesus that the earthly singers could not sing.

All through these readings we must have been thinking of the rough simplicity of the birth of the Son of God. We might have expected that, if he had to be born in this world at all, it would be in a palace or mansion. There was a European monarch who worried his court by often disappearing and walking incognito amongst his people. When he was asked not to do so for security's sake, he answered, 'I cannot rule my people unless I know how they live'. It is a great thought of the Christian faith that we have a God who knows the life we live because he too lived it and claimed no special advantage over common people.

William Barclay
The Gospel of Luke

The birth of Jesus is the centre of Christmas. What one learns about Jesus from the narratives that relate his birth comes, however, from the actions and words of the other characters of Christmas – in Luke, from the shepherds, the angelic messenger, the heavenly chorus, the mysterious bystanders (Luke 2:18), and Mary; in Matthew, from repeated angelic messengers, Joseph, the Wise Men, Herod, the chief priests and scribes. Nowhere is that more evident than in the Lukan story, where a bare statement of the birth of Jesus is followed by the intriguing account of the nameless shepherds. They are traced from their location in the field tending their flock through their visit to Bethlehem and back to where they originated. From their actions and their interactions with the angelic messenger and the heavenly host, we learn about the character and significance of Jesus' birth.

We first meet the shepherds doing what shepherds are supposed to be doing – tending their flocks. They no doubt remind Luke's readers of the shepherding done once in these same regions by Jesus' famous ancestor, David. The routineness of these shepherds' lives is abruptly interrupted by the appearance of the angelic messenger. Their world, circumscribed at night by the wandering of the sheep, is exploded by the awesome presence of this one who brings news of Jesus' birth. The manifestation of the divine glory, the shepherds' fright, the announcement of the messenger, disrupt their order and uniformity and set them on a journey to hear and see earth-changing events.

Three things we note about the intrusive announcement of the messenger. First, the good news includes great joy for 'all the people'. It is not merely the shepherds' small world that is changed by the word of Jesus' birth, but it is Israel's world. While Luke sets the story of the birth in the context of the Roman Empire (2:1-2), he has a primary interest in the destiny of Israel and 'the falling and the rising of many' for whom this baby is sent (verse 34). Jesus' relevance for the world, in fact, begins in the city of David as the fulfilment of Jewish expectations. It includes the acceptance of Jewish traditions (verses 21, 22-40, 41-52), and only from this very particular origin does its universal character emerge.

Second, the announcement focuses on three astounding titles this baby is to carry – Saviour, Messiah, and Lord. 'Saviour' has meaning in the narrative because the original readers would recognise that such a title the exalted Emperor Augustus had borne. Unfortunately, the eager anticipations for a brighter, more peaceful day stirred by his rule were long since dashed by the brutality and weakness of his successors.

Now a true and promise-fulfilling Saviour appears. 'Messiah' (or 'Christ') reminds us of Israel's hope for the anointed figure and God's grand design which he will inaugurate. 'Lord', interestingly, occurs four times in our passage, and in the other three instances is used for God (2:9 [twice], 15). It is inescapable in such a context, then, that divine associations be attached to Jesus (in verse 11).

Third, the angelic announcement designates the sign that will assure the shepherds that they have found 'a Saviour, who is the Messiah, the Lord'. But such a strange sign! Hardly fitting for one bearing such honoured titles! The babe 'wrapped in bands of cloth and lying in a manger', however, is only the beginning of the story of God's unusual ways in accomplishing the divine rule. Not by might or coercive tactics, but in submission and humbleness, Jesus fulfills his vocation.

Perhaps it is the perplexity caused by such a menial sign for such an exalted baby that evokes the immediate confirmation of the heavenly chorus, who join the angelic messenger in a doxology. God is praised for the birth of this child because the birth begins God's reign of peace on earth. The creatures of the heavenly world, in a context of praise, announce God's good plans for this world.

Having heard the heavenly witnesses, the shepherds now decide to go to Bethlehem and 'see' this revelation. Like other disciples who abruptly leave fishing boats and tax tables, they go 'with haste'. We are not told what happened to the flocks, apparently left in the fields. The shepherds' old world has been shattered by the appearance of the messenger, and now they are in search of a new one, one centred in the event that has occurred in Bethlehem.

When the shepherds find Mary, Joseph, and Jesus, the narrator records that they report the message that had been made known to them about the baby. To whom did they give their report? To Mary and Joseph? Perhaps. Perhaps the shepherds, in responding to the angelic messenger in fact became a confirmation to Mary and Joseph of the significance of this baby so unusually born. But there must have been a wider audience for the shepherds' report too, since 'all who heard it' were astonished – not believing or thoughtful or adoring, just 'amazed'. Apparently nothing spurred them to ask questions or pursue the matter further. In contrast, Mary clings to what has happened. She continues to ponder the events and the words (the Greek word is inclusive of both) of the shepherds' visit.

Finally, the shepherds go back to where they came from, apparently back to fields and to flocks, but not back to business as usual. What was told them by the angelic messenger has been confirmed. They have heard and seen for themselves. Their old world is gone, replaced by a new world. Whatever the structure and order of life before, their world is now centred in the praise and glorifying of God. The nights in the field will never be the same.

Beverly R. Gaventa
Texts for Preaching

Second Sunday of Christmas

John 1:(1-9) 10-18

You know, we're really not creatures of darkness.
Just as an animal creeps into the dark to die, so I suppose a man makes for the light. He wants to die at home, and the darkness is never home to us.

On Sunday, 31 January 1971 Commander Alan Shepherd along with his two colleagues, Stu Roosa and Ed Mitchell, blasted off in Apollo 14 on their way to the moon. Their command module was called Kitty Hawk and the landing module Antares.

On Saturday, 6 February, five days, 9 hours 53 minutes of elapsed time after lift-off, while Stu Roosa was alone in the command module with Shepherd and Mitchell in Antares on the moon's surface, this event took place:

As Kitty Hawk drifted silently through the realm of earth-light, the cabin cooled slightly – just a few degrees at first, but that was enough that the environmental control system could not remove all the moisture in the air. Then the spacecraft went out of radio contact and into total, unyielding darkness. He liked the solitude, but he couldn't deny the feeling of loneliness. His only company was the stars that filled the sky, except where the moon blotted out even these distant companions. While Roosa worked the air turned clammy, and suddenly it seemed he could *feel* the darkness. He knew in that moment what it was to be utterly alone.

After nearly a half-hour of this – longer than most previous missions, because the landing site was well to the west, and most of the near side was in sunlight – something remarkable happened. In a finger snap, the cabin was flooded with sunlight, and it was such a glorious feeling of renewal, even rebirth, that Roosa said to himself, 'You know, we're really not creatures of darkness'. Roosa realised where he was and felt great and small at the same time. It was the moon that made him feel big: he'd made it all the way out here. And it was the sight of the earth – now, for Roosa, an object of undeniable wonder and nostalgia – that made him feel small.

Andrew Chaikin
A Man on the Moon: The Voyages of the Apollo Astronauts

Harry Lime *(The Third Man)* sold watered-down penicillin in postwar Vienna at inflated prices. He is finally hunted down by his best friend Rollo Martin who shoots and wounds him in an underground sewer. Harry tries desperately to climb some steps leading to a manhole in the street and so to the light.

Harry 'was in great pain, and just as an animal creeps into the dark to die, so I suppose a man makes for the light. He wants to die at home, and the darkness is never home to us.'

Graham Greene
The Third Man

'Enough!' said God. 'Enough. We have heard enough.'

'But have we heard the Truth?' said God's Son. He still had no idea what the Truth might be.

'No, not the Truth,' said God sadly. 'Not the Truth.'

'Then tell us the Truth,' said God's Son.

'What is the Truth?'

All the misty glowing shapes of the people on the grass were watching God, whose face now seemed brighter than ever.

'What is the Truth?' cried God's Son, insistent.

'The Truth,' said God finally, 'is this. The Truth is that I was those Worms.'

God's Son stared at his Father, looking blank.

'And the Truth is,' God went on, 'that I was that Fox. Just as I was that Foal. As I am, I am. I am that Foal. And I am that Cow. I am the Weasel and the Mouse. The Wood Pigeon and the Partridge. The Goat, the Badger, the Hedgehog, the Hare. Yes and the Hedgehog's Flea. I am each of these things. The Rat. The Fly. And each of these things is Me. It is. That is the Truth.'

God's Son remembered all that had been said about these creatures and he stared at the misty shapes of the souls on the grass, and under his gaze the shapes began to fade.

'Don't go away,' cried God's Son. 'Stay a moment. Did you hear all that? Did you know the Truth about all these creatures?'

But as he spoke they thinned, until they were no more than faint wraiths of mist creeping along the hillsides. And God's Son saw the oak leaves move, and felt on his cheek a slight chill of the air.

He turned and saw that his Father had disappeared. Instead the sky was very bright under a long low cloud in the east. And the middle of that cloud glowed like the gilded lintel of a doorway that had been rubbed bright.

Then God's Son hesitated. It occurred to him, with a little shiver, that he was where he had wanted to be. He stood on the earth. And below him he could see the roofs of the farm. And there in the early mist was the village, and beyond it in every direction, other farms, where the people still slept, but where the cocks were already beginning to crow.

Ted Hughes
What is the truth?

Planet Earth

God was sitting in his garden, in the evening with his gin
(for the joys of creativity were wearing rather thin).
He had drafted out the universe, and calculated Pi,
then he saw a barren, blue-green ball suspended in the sky.
'I'll create a whole new planet with high mountains and
    deep seas
and a billion different life forms from great dinosaurs to trees,
and the balance will be perfect, Nature's harmony complete –
until I create a primate that walks upright, on two feet.
These said creatures shall be jealous – they'll make wars and
    want to fight,
they will have a sense of logic, so they can't tell wrong from
    right.
Out of all the different life forms there, they'll be the most
    confused,
with their things they call "society" and even "moral views".
I shall colour them in every hue, from black to milky white,
they'll play games of "race relations" and of "basic human
    rights",
and so they haven't got a hope of knowing what to do,
I shall make them eleven sexes but say there are only two.
I will give them "state economies" and drugs to dull their
    minds,
so that they think they know about the safety of mankind,
while their world expires around them, and the sands of
    time run dry,

while the piles of deadly weapons rear against the clear blue
    sky.'
Then God broke off, for the thought did not somehow appeal
    to him,
of a planet's own destruction – so he polished off his gin.
But the thought was not forgotten, for, before the sun had set,
God had catalogued Earth's blueprint in his filing cabinet.
And, there, on his coloured memo pad (with ballpoint, done
    in red)
the clear headline 'Eve and Adam' could quite obviously be
    read.

Sarah Sarkhel, aged 16 years
Quoted in *Liturgy of Life* by Donald Hilton

Necessary elements

Whatever happens the general oversight of the creation must continue; the Father must remain the Father. If there is a breakdown on the human side a precise work is called for, which includes pardon, power and price. The final limits will be stretched as much as in the creative act itself; it is a kind of new creation, a life and death issue. A variety of measures of increasing weight could be brought into play, but there is always the possibility that the extremest measures might be called for, and thus provision to the utmost must be reckoned for. Sacrifice, pain, patience, creative love in some final, decisive, and universal act may be required. There must be an entrance into the conflict, a bearing of the consequences in terms of physical, moral, emotional expenditure and endurance, as part of a clear and wholeheartedly accepted plan, with preparatory stages, a ripe time, a prepared follow up, a concluding climax, of which the whole turning point will be at once the core and the clue of the whole business. 'The Lamb was slain from the foundation of the world' (Revelation 13:8 cf 22:1-3). The incarnation is part of the cross, and both reflect the nature and purpose of the Creator of the universe, which was so constructed that God was free to enter the limits of his own world without being finally conquered by them. The ground plan of the universe is cruciform. The roots of the cross are fast within our fairest fields, as Francis Thompson put it.

T. D. Meadley
Top Level Talks

45

The Epiphany

Matthew 2:1-12

*It was for love,
because of love,
impelled by love's
heartache, that I
crossed deserts. . . .
For in my heart
there was indeed
a great love, a love
compatible with
incense, because it
aspired to flower
in worship.*

The Journey of the Magi

'A cold coming we had of it,
just the worst time of the year
for a journey.
And such a long journey.
The ways deep and the weather sharp,
the very dead of winter.'

If I were to ask you which member of Gray's Inn wrote those most apposite Epiphany lines, I'm sure most of you would say: 'Ah, *The Journey of the Magi* – T. S. Eliot.' And you'd be quite right. But T. S. Eliot – like some preachers I know! – wasn't above lifting a good quotation when he saw one. And those particular lines he lifted, with hardly a word of amendment, from one of the greatest sermons in English literature, preached before the King's Majesty at Whitehall on Christmas Day, 1622 by Bishop Lancelot Andrewes, whose commemorative window is on the north side of our chapel.

I would like simply to read, first of all, a few paragraphs from that most marvellous sermon:

'It was no summer progress. A cold coming they had of it, at this time of the year, just the worst time of the year to make a journey, and specially a long journey, in. The ways deep, the weather sharp, the days short, the sun farthest off, in *solstitio brumali*, the very dead of winter . . .

'And these difficulties they overcame, of a wearisome, irksome, troublesome, dangerous, unseasonable journey; and for all this, they came. And came it cheerfully and quickly, as appeareth by the speed they made. It was *vidimus, venimus*, with them – they saw and they came; no sooner saw, but they set out presently. So as upon the first appearing of the star, as it might be last night, they knew it was Balaam's star; it called them away; they made ready straight to begin their journey that morning. A sign they were highly conceited of his birth, believed some great matter of it, that they took all those pains, made all this haste, that they might be there to worship him with all possible speed they could. Sorry for nothing so much that they could not be there soon enough, with the very first, to do it even this day, the day of his birth . . .

'And we, what should we have done? Sure these men of

the East shall rise in judgement against the men of the West, that is us, and their faith against ours in this point. With them it was but *vidimus, venimus*; with us it would have been but *veniemus* at most; our fashion is to see and see again before we stir a foot, especially if it be to the worship of Christ. Come such a journey at such a time? No; but fairly have put it off to the spring of the year, till the days longer, and the ways fairer, and the weather warmer, till better travelling to Christ. Our Epiphany would sure have fallen in Easter week at the soonest.'

Eric James
Judge not: A Selection of Sermons

The legend of the Magi who came from the East to worship the infant Jesus derives from just a few lines in St Matthew's Gospel; and yet it is one of the most potent episodes in the Christian tradition. Who were these foreign kings? What brought them to Bethlehem, and what did they find there?

Michel Tournier offers answers to these questions in his new novel, as he brings Gaspar, Melchior and Balthasar vividly to life. Each tells the story of how he lost what he loved most; Gaspar, the black king, deserted by his white slave mistress; Melchior, lover of wealth and power, who has been deposed; and Balthasar, patron of the arts, robbed of his precious collections . . . (From the flyleaf of *The Four Wise Men.*) To these three traditional Wise Men, Tournier adds a fourth one called Prince Taor who arrives too late for the Nativity.

'When we told him about the star and our quest, King Herod, who had consulted his priests, informed us that Bethlehem was the goal of our journey. For the prophet Micah had written: "And thou Bethlehem in the land of Judah, thou art not the least among the princes of Judah, for out of thee shall come a Governor that shall rule my people." To the three questions we had brought with us he added one of his own that had been tormenting him on the threshold of death, the question of his succession. To that question as well as ours, he said, Bethlehem must supply the answer. And he charged us as his plenipotentiaries to identify this heir, and then to bring him word in Jerusalem. We intended to do his bidding in all loyalty; we didn't want it said that this tyrant, who had been flouted and deceived throughout his reign, every one of whose crimes can be explained if not justified by an act of treachery, had on his deathbed been betrayed by foreign kings whom he had entertained magnificently. But then the Angel Gabriel, who had played the majordomo of the stable, begged us to go straight home without passing through Jerusalem, because, as he said, Herod was nourishing dark designs with regard to the child. I talked it over with the other princes: What were we to do? I thought we should keep our promise. Not only as a matter of honour, but because we knew what lengths the King of the Jews could go to when he thought himself betrayed. By reporting to him in Jerusalem, I argued, we could allay his suspicion and forestall great misfortunes. But Gaspar and Balthasar insisted on doing Gabriel's bidding. "For once an archangel tells us what to do!" they cried out. They were two against one, and I was the youngest and poorest, so in the end I gave in. But I regret it, and I think I shall never forgive myself. And now, Prince Taor, I've told you how, having approached the powerful, I feel soiled for all time.'

'But then you went to Bethlehem. What did Bethlehem teach you about power?'

'By the example of the crib, the Archangel Gabriel, who was watching over the child, taught me the strength of weakness, the irresistible gentleness of the non-violent, the law of forgiveness, which does not abolish the law of *talion* (retaliation) but infinitely transcends it. For *talion* prescribes that the vengeance must not exceed the offence. It is a way station between natural anger and perfect concord. The Kingdom of God will never be established once and for all. The key to it must be forged slowly, and we ourselves are that key. In view of all this, I laid the gold coin struck with the effigy of my father King Theodenos at the child's feet. It was my only treasure, my only proof that I was the legal heir to the throne of Palmyra. In relinquishing it, I renounced the kingdom to search for that other kingdom promised me by the Saviour. I shall withdraw into the desert with my faithful Baktiar. We shall found a community with all those who wish to join us. It will be the first city of God. There we shall meditate in the expectation of his coming. A community of free men with no other law but the law of love . . .'

He turned to Gaspar, who was on his left.

'I have just uttered the word "love". But how can I fail to recognise that my African brother has a far better, purer and more compelling right than I to speak of that great, mysterious emotion? For wasn't it for love, King Gaspar, that you left your capital city and travelled so far northward?'

'Yes,' said Gaspar, King of Meroe, 'it was for love, because of love, impelled by love's heartache, that I crossed deserts. But you mustn't suppose that I ran away from a woman who didn't love me, or that I was trying to forget an unhappy love. If I had thought that, Bethlehem would have taught me otherwise. To make it clear, I shall have to take you back . . . back to the incense, to the use I made of incense one night when we – the woman I loved, her lover, and I – were clowning to amuse ourselves. We had painted our faces grotesquely, and smoke rising from censers enveloped us in fragrance. I have no doubt that the combination of sacred smoke with that degrading scene contributed to opening my eyes. I realised; what did I realise? That I should have to go away, I'm sure of that. But the deeper meaning of my journey dawned on me only when I saw the child. For in my heart there was indeed a great love, a love compatible with incense, because it aspired to flower in worship. . . . In reality, I myself was weeping over an unappeased love. With each passing day I found Biltine weaker, lazier, stupider, more deceitful and frivolous. To cleanse her of all this wretched humanity I'd have needed an immense, inexhaustibly generous heart. At least I never held it up to her. I knew that I myself, that my own soul-lessness was to blame for the poverty of our adventure. I didn't have enough love for both of us, that's all! I ought to have irrigated her cold, dry, calculating heart with luminous tenderness, and I couldn't. What the child taught me – but I had guessed as much, my heart had an intimation of the lesson – was that a love that is worship is *always* shared, because its radiance makes it irresistibly communicative. When I approached the crib I laid the coffer of incense at the child's feet, for he is the only being on earth deserving of that sacred homage. I knelt down. I touched my fingers to my lips and threw the child a kiss. He smiled. He held out his arms to me. Then I knew the perfect encounter between the lover and the beloved for what it was: this tremulous veneration, this jubilant hymn, this marvelling fascination . . .

And there was something more, which for me, Gaspar of Meroe, surpassed all the rest in beauty – a miraculous surprise which the Holy Family had obviously prepared in the expectation of my coming.'

'What was that surprise, King Gaspar? I am consumed with perplexity and impatience.'

'Very well, I shall tell you. Balthasar told you just now that he believed in the existence of a black Adam, the Adam of before the Fall, and that only the other Adam, the Adam of sin was white.'

'I have indeed heard a passing allusion to the black Adam from his lips.'

'At first I thought Balthasar had said that to give me

pleasure. He is so kind! But in bending over the crib to adore the child, what do I see? A black baby with kinky hair, with a sweet flat nose, in short, a baby just like the African babies of my country.'

'First a black Adam, then a black Jesus!'

'Isn't it logical? If Adam didn't turn white until after he had sinned, mustn't Jesus in his original state be black like our ancestors?'

'But what about his parents? Mary and Joseph?'

'White, I assure you! As white as Melchior and Balthasar!'

'I shall share Bethlehem's marvellous lesson of love with all who are willing to listen to me.'

'Good. Begin with Prince Taor. Give me my first lesson in Christian love.'

'The child in the crib, who became black, the better to welcome Gaspar, the African king. There's more love in that than in all the love stories I know. That beautiful image teaches us to become like those we love, to see with their eyes, to speak their mother tongue, to *respect* them, a word which originally meant *to look at twice*. Thus exalted, pleasure, joy and happiness fuse into love.

If you expect another to give you pleasure or joy, does it mean that you love him? No. You love only yourself. You want him to serve your self-love. True love is the pleasure we get from another's pleasure, the joy that springs up in us at the sight of his joy, the happiness it gives me to know that he is happy. Pleasure from pleasure, joy from joy, happiness from happiness – that is love, nothing more.'

Michel Tournier
The Four Wise Men

First Sunday of Epiphany
The Baptism of the Lord/Ordinary Time 1

Mark 1:4-11

His baptism is Christ's commitment to his vocation: his awful vocation.

From time to time I like to renew and refresh my own understanding of the sacrament of baptism. I did it this week by paying one of my periodic visits to the National Gallery, and simply standing once again in front of one of my favourite paintings: *The Baptism of Christ* by Piero della Francesca.

Piero was born in the Umbrian town of San Sepolcro in about the year 1410. He showed an early talent for mathematics, but in due course it was decided that he would be a painter.

To be a painter, in those days, was to be a tradesman or craftsman. Piero was employed at the princely courts of central Italy, and at Rome, but in about 1460 he lost his sight, and from then on he lived in San Sepolcro, and devoted himself entirely to mathematics and the theory of perspective. These subjects were almost obsessive preoccupations for him throughout his life, and play an enormously important part in his paintings.

Most probably, Piero painted his *Baptism of Christ* in about 1440, for the Camaldolite Abbey, later the Cathedral, of Borgo San Sepolcro: as part of an altar piece, appropriately for its altar dedicated to St John the Baptist.

Although the fifteenth century was a period of great intellectual advance, it was also one of all but universal illiteracy; and it was one of the artist's chief tasks to tell the story so that it would be easily intelligible and act as a substitute for the written word for those unable to read.

'Every picture tells a story.' And Piero's *Baptism of Christ* certainly does. By means of painting, he introduces us to the heights and depths of Christian truth.

Piero's approach to the biblical account is literal and precise; and the moment he has chosen to portray is sufficiently specific to show that it's clearly St Luke's Gospel which is in mind, for St John the Baptist is in the very act of baptising Jesus: and Jesus is bringing his hands together, on the point of beginning his prayer, while the dove hovers above his head.

Piero has taken enormous pains to represent every detail from the Gospel that is capable of being shown visually, and has included hardly anything that is superfluous to it. Almost every detail has a specific symbolic or narrative part to play.

There's, for instance, a figure to the right, in the middle ground, struggling with his shirt as he takes it off, getting ready to be baptised. Clearly Piero means us to set Christ's baptism alongside the baptism of others.

The whole of the left side of the painting is dominated by a huge overhanging tree, which clearly refers to that passage in St Luke in which John the Baptist says: 'Now also the axe is laid unto the root of the tree: every tree therefore which bringeth not forth good fruit is hewn down and cast into the fire.' And you can see the stumps of trees that have already been hewn down!

What a warning to those who are taking upon themselves the responsibilities of baptism!

As you look at the painting, you are confronted by the literally central figure of the praying Christ: praying as he stands ready to be baptised. But perhaps even more dominant, and as central as the figure of Christ, is the mysterious haunting presence of the dove: hovering, floating above the Christ: the core of both the story and the painting. It's in many ways the most real thing in the picture: unnaturally white and radiant. Of course, it's above the head of Christ, and yet it seems so still, in mid-air, that it seems to lose the kind of earth-bound location that everything else has. It's more apparition than physical reality; the dove descending as a ghost: the Holy Ghost. (It's a tall order to paint the Holy Ghost!)

I've said that Piero paints in order to tell the story for the illiterate; but it would be wrong to say it's simply a simple telling of the story. It's clear that to Piero the truth is never simple.

Look at the face of Christ and you see a seriousness and solemnity that betokens a moment of the utmost importance. It's the baptism of Christ, and nothing more, the artist seems to say – but adds: and nothing less. His baptism is Christ's commitment to his vocation: his awful vocation.

Piero's paintings are often said to have an extraordinary quality of stillness about them. Christ praying is still. The dove hovering is, nevertheless, still. The water, pouring from the shell onto Christ's head, is still. It's a moment in time, a very special moment in time, 'captured' as we say; but it's also a moment in eternity. Obviously it's not intended to suggest the event lasted for ever; but it does suggest that it's valid for ever.

Eric James
Judge not: A Selection of Sermons

Second Sunday of Epiphany
Ordinary Time 2

John 1:43-51

Revelation in the biblical sense is never open and obvious to everyone, interested or not, believer or not. There is always about it a kind of radiant obscurity, a concealing that requires faith to grasp the revealing.

After spending an exhilarating, exhausting and hectic five years in ministry in Birmingham working closely with the Boys Brigade and broadcasting regularly on what was then BBC Radio Birmingham, I decided that a change into a lower gear and less frenetic lifestyle and ministry was what I needed. So I accepted an invitation to 'Glorious Devon'.

There I found the pace of life much slower and I was even told to slow down when recording my first talk for the BBC in Plymouth. I was using the usual fast pace required by Radio Birmingham, but the producer stopped me short and said, 'Slow down, you're in the West Country now'. And I must say I was deeply grateful for the slower pace.

My primary task was to build a new church in a small Devon market town. The site straddled two large housing developments, one private and the other council, with the church building commanding a wonderful view of Dartmoor; Haytor, Saddletor and Houndtor could be clearly seen on a fine day through a church window and from the spacious car park.

I was fortunate also in that a new manse was built at the opposite end of the car park from the church. From our garden patio, we also had some superb views of Dartmoor and many memorable sunsets did we glory in.

After some time I received an invitation to meet with police, social workers, probation officers and other community workers to discuss common problems.

We had an excellent lunch and afterwards one of the delegates asked me who I was and where I lived. When I told him, he laughed out loud and said, 'Can any good person come from that area?' He then looked scornfully at me and walked off, never to speak to me again.

That incident powerfully reminded me of the Gospel for today where Philip finds Nathanael and says to him: 'We have found him of whom Moses in the law and also the prophets wrote, Jesus of Nazareth, the son of Joseph.' Nathanael's retort is, 'Can anything good come out of Nazareth?' Very wisely, Philip does not try and argue the case. He says simply, 'Come and see'.

Ron Dale

The biblical word central to the season of Epiphany is *revelation*, for this is the time to celebrate the revealing of the Son of God. But the companion word to revelation is *witness*, for revelation in the biblical sense is never open and obvious to everyone, interested or not, believer or not. There is always about it a kind of radiant obscurity, a concealing that requires faith to grasp the revealing. One is not permitted a controlled, managed, guaranteed, no-risk response to Jesus. Those, therefore, who have beheld the glory become flesh (John 1:14) cannot prove, but they can witness. Witnessing to the revelation does not refer to lengthy self-disclosures, narrating one's feelings in response to the word, but rather to confession of what one has seen and heard. No one understands this better than the author of the fourth Gospel who, after a prologue announcing the revelation (John 1:1-18), follows with a series of accounts of witnessing to Jesus Christ (John 1:19-51).

In the Gospel of John, witnessing to Christ begins with John the Baptist (1:29-34). Verses 19-28 are primarily John's witness about himself, that he is not the Christ. John's testimony causes two of his disciples to follow Jesus (verses 35-42), and they in turn witness to their friends (verses 43-51), creating an ever widening circle of testimony.

Our reading for today belongs, then, to this widening circle of witness and faith – a circle that, as we shall see at verse 51, includes the reader of this Gospel. The author has already spoken *for* the community of faith ('we have seen his glory', John 1:14) but at the close of this text, he will speak *to* the reader as a member of the community.

The record begins in a clear, straightforward way. The place is Bethsaida in Galilee, and the witness is Philip, having recently been called to faith by Jesus, and the listener is Nathanael. The word to Nathanael is faith's witness to Jesus as the promised Messiah. The response is a reasonable one: the credentials of Jesus hardly qualify him as the one promised by Moses and the prophets as the people's deliverer. Those of us who regularly evaluate strangers by place of origin, residence, family, education, and station should not find Nathanael's response unusual. The invitation to join in faith's enquiry is extended: 'Come and see' (verse 46; also 1:39; 4:29; 11:34). Let the preacher notice that witnessing invites, it does not argue or coerce, and certainly does not cartoon or discredit Nathanael's initial doubt. Faith sickens and dies in an atmosphere where doubt is laughed at. Nathanael encounters Jesus' supernatural knowledge and is persuaded. (Recall the Samaritan woman's response to Jesus' special knowledge about her, John 4:16-19.)

Nathanael's confession of faith (verse 49) seems too elaborate, too enormous, to have been prompted solely by Jesus' words to him. Clearly, Nathanael is voicing the community's faith. In fact, as 'truly an Israelite', who is never mentioned in the lists of Jesus' disciples in the other Gospels and Acts, he could be a paradigm of believing Israel, those within Judaism who accepted Jesus as Messiah. Such a view is supported by the identification of Jesus with Jacob (who became Israel) at Bethel (Genesis 28:12). Angels descending and ascending as at Bethel (verse 51), dramatically identify Jesus as the place of God's presence. In him heaven and earth are joined; he is 'the gate of heaven'. In John's language, the Word made flesh reveals God's glory . . .

Thus a simple story of a person meeting Jesus is elaborated into a Christian proclamation. Clear evidence of this is found in the shift to the plural form of 'you' in the dominical saying in verse 51: 'Very truly, I tell you, you will see.' That which began as private conversation is now obviously sermonic: Jesus speaks to all, including the readers. (See the same move from private to public through the shift to the plural 'you' in Jesus' conversation with Nicodemus (John 3:1ff., especially verses 7, 11, 12). The observant preacher will find in this form of literary movement (from conversation to proclamation) a pattern of communication that is both effective and congenial to a Gospel that does not pound the listener into a choiceless corner. Notice also that verses 50-51 include the readers, living as they do at a time and distance from Galilee, within the circle of Jesus' followers. In fact, rather than be at a disadvantage as though they were second-hand believers, the readers (including us) will, because of faith, see even 'greater things than these'.

Fred B. Craddock
Preaching Through the Christian Year: 'B'

Third Sunday of Epiphany*
Ordinary Time 3

Mark 1:14-20 (RCL)

The idea of call or vocation remains at the heart of the Christian gospel. What does the idea of call mean to you?

Intuition

The central theme at the beginning of Jesus' ministry is the call of the first disciples. The idea of call or vocation remains at the heart of the Christian gospel. What does the idea of call mean to you?

Look back over your own experiences. Have you been aware of a call from God, and in what form has such a call been expressed? Perhaps very few Christians claim to hear the divine voice call their names and speak out their future direction. But perhaps the call comes in other ways, in ways more diverse and more subtle.

Why, for example, are you a follower of Jesus today? Did you seek him out and hunt him down? Or did he seek you out and prompt the initial stirrings of your religious quest?

Can you, for example, point to a major encounter which proved decisive in your pilgrimage of life? Did Jesus rock your boat and suddenly challenge you to follow him? Or has your experience been less dramatic than that? Can you point to a growing certainty or just a developing inevitability of it all? Once Jesus begins to pull the heart-strings or pushes on the rudder of your life, it may be incredibly difficult to get away or to ignore the steering.

Or how are you aware of that call today? Are you in a mood to be responsive to the promptings of the Lord? Are you willing to let certain things go and to leave certain things behind? Are you willing to become a new person in the service of the Lord? Or do you prefer to stay put, to hold fast, and to hope that the call will go away?

Feeling

Put yourself into one of those two fishing boats and try to see how things felt for the men inside. Become Peter, Andrew, James or John and identify with their feelings. On

*See page 60 for a reading related to John 2:1-11 (CWL Gospel reading).

the outside they are ordinary folk doing an ordinary job. On the outside they are simple fishermen. On the inside, however, they are sophisticated and complex individuals. We shall, of course, never know what was going on in their lives on that eventful day. But we can imagine and feel.

We can imagine and feel their personal anxieties and concerns. The catch had not been good. The nets were wearing thin. The mortgage on the boat was overdue. The aged father was infirm. The mother-in-law was sick. We can imagine and feel their personal hopes and plans. A new style of net will increase the yield. Father's retirement will provide opportunity to try new techniques. Their own boys are nearly ripe for joining the family business.

On the outside they make a simple, positive and direct decision. On the outside they simply abandon the past and set sights on a new future. On the inside, however, they are human beings wrestling with enormous decisions and accepting huge consequences. . . . But more than this, we need to imagine and feel the implications for those left behind. We can imagine and feel the impact of the young fishermen's decisions on the ageing parents, as their own security and old age was being eroded. Even Simon's mother-in-law must have been disadvantaged by Simon's abrupt departure. We can imagine and feel the impact of the young fishermen's decisions on their wives and children.

And we must ask just how responsible Jesus was being in disrupting family life so violently.

Thinking

The key question for the theologian concerned with gospel studies is this. Why did Mark choose to open his gospel narrative with the account of the call of four disciples, rather than by relating some of the words of teaching or the acts of healing which would logically lead to people wishing to follow him?

The answer is that this opening call set the *structure* for what is to follow. Mark's primary interest is in showing how Jesus constructed round him a new Israel, a new people of God. The clue is given by the way in which the call of the first four followers (Peter, Andrew, James and John) is followed by the call of a fifth follower (Levi). Then there is a general commissioning of the twelve special disciples. The twelve are named and Levi is dropped from the list. The same thing, you see, so often happens in the Old Testament when the twelve tribes of Israel are named. There, too, Levi is often dropped from the list and the number twelve is kept alive by counting separately the two sons of Joseph, namely Ephraim and Manasseh. Mark's intention is clear.

For Mark, the words of teaching and the works of healing are not there to attract the twelve followers, but to equip them. The teaching and the healing are the object lessons from which they are to learn. Then having learnt, they themselves are sent out to teach and heal, the very activities which bear witness to the fact that the kingdom of God has come near. Where God reigns, the words of the kingdom and the new life of the kingdom are free for all to receive.

For Mark, therefore, the call of the first disciples is, indeed, the proper opening act for the Jesus who comes proclaiming, 'The time is fulfilled, and the kingdom of God has come near'.

Leslie J. Francis
Personality Type and Scripture: Exploring Mark's Gospel

One of the most influential people of the eighteenth century was John Wesley, Anglican cleric and leader, with his brother Charles, of the great spiritual awakening that happened during their lifetime. Here is a flavour of John, taken from the Prefatory Note found in volume three of his Journal:

'In the present volume Wesley appears as preacher, writer, controversialist, educator. He preaches, often every day of the week, morning, noon and night, wherever a crowd can gather or his voice can be heard. His printers are never idle, nor are his literary foes. Books, tracts, letters, hymns, pamphlets pour from the press in a ceaseless stream. But beyond and above all else he is a leader and commander. He compels. The people are charmed by a strange personality. His hand, his eye, the tone of his voice, cast spells about the wildest. All sorts and conditions hate him savagely or love him passionately. They wonder and fear as at one sent from God; but almost invariably they follow and obey. The life of such a man, incessantly travelling, often traversing swiftly flowing currents of national movement, appeals to the romanticist, for it is rich in startling situations and thrilling episodes. But still more powerfully it appeals to the historian, for he cannot fail to see in it one of those moral and spiritual forces that make history.'

Wednesday, 26 October 1743

I enlarged upon those deep words, 'Repent and believe the Gospel'. When I had done a man stood forth in the midst, one who had exceedingly troubled his brethren, vehemently maintaining (for the plague had spread hither also) that they ought not to pray, to sing, to communicate, to search the Scriptures or to trouble themselves about works, but only to believe and be still; and said, with a loud voice, 'Mr Wesley, let me speak a few words. Is it not said, "A certain man had two sons: and he said unto the younger, 'Go work today in my vineyard': and he answered, 'I will not'; but afterwards he repented and went?" I am he. I said yesterday, "I will not go to hear him; I will have nothing to do with him". But I repent. Here is my hand. By the grace of God, I will not leave you as long as I live.'

John Wesley
The Journal of John Wesley: Vol. 3

Third Sunday of Epiphany
Ordinary Time 3

John 2:1-11 (CWL)

Alive to your world, alive to your God: with such life you can be alive to each other.

Humour, wonder, and the other

Every Catholic wedding has a built-in paradox. The paradox is not the bride and groom; the paradox is the preacher. On the one hand, a confirmed batchelor is not your prime choice for marriage counsellor. . . . I am a coach who never got into the game. On the other hand, I've been a wedlock watcher for seven decades, from the wedded life of my father and mother to the marriages of the 1980s with their 50 per cent casualty rate. It is from this lengthy, if limited, experience that three sets of ideas have just recently jelled, three qualities a man and woman must share if they are to live in love for life as man and wife . . .

What three gifts do you need, next year and the next fifty? First, a sense of humour; second, a sense of wonder; third, a sense of the other. A word on each.

To begin with, you need a sense of humour. I don't mean you can recognise a raunchy joke. More profoundly, you can discover, appreciate, express what is comical or incongruous, absurd or ridiculous, in an idea, an event, a situation – even a person. [You] act out what the novelist Thackeray put so well: Humour is 'a mixture of love and wit'.

So then, my first medicine for the married is laughter. Not always, of course. You do not laugh at cancer or a coronary, make merry over famine in Ethiopia. It means that you take yourself seriously, but not too seriously. You see and smile at or roar over the little and large absurdities in your make-up: the strange creature who believes and doubts, hopes and fears, loves and hates – afraid of your joy, feeling bad if you feel good. You see and smile at the faults and foibles in the other half – from the way he slurps his [coffee] to the time she takes to put on her face. And you can look at the world together with light laughter, amused at the absurd all around you. Oh, not arrogant or supercilious or haughty or proud. Simply aware that life out there, if at times grim, can only be lived humanly if you see it for the contradiction it is: a world where men and women kill one another and die for one another, where the angel and the devil in all of us vie for supremacy, where so much of our time is taken up with the superficial, where men don't weep because it's weak and womanly, where people work themselves into ulcers to have fun, play games to get ahead, to be liked, to be admired, where to be in fashion is to re-create yourself from head to foot in line with the gospel according to TV.

If laughter can sometimes save a life . . . it can save a marriage. In a recent editorial in the *Journal of the American Medical Association*, humourist Art Buchwald admitted that there are 'many unanswered questions': Can you laugh yourself to death? If laughter is such good medicine, why will not Medicare or Medicaid pay for it? Can you transplant a sense of humour? And much scientific work remains to be done 'before the Food and Drug Administration will permit [laughter] to be used in large doses'. Nevertheless, a fascinating fact remains; I've seen it time and time again. Prescription number one for a healthy marriage is a sense of humour: to see the incongruous in yourself, in the other, in the world, talk wittily about it, laugh lovingly over it. A mixture of love and wit.

Second, you need a sense of wonder. I don't mean curiosity, perplexity, doubt. I mean that, even after a quarter of a century on this paradoxical planet, you two can still be surprised, delighted, amazed. Amazed at what? Amazed at being alive.

Alive, first, to your world – a world outside and inside. Amazed that with a flicker of eyelids you can span a universe, from an amoeba to outer space; you can open your ears to a skylark or Michael Jackson, smell the scents of Chicago, feast your taste buds with lasagna or ice cream, touch a face or a flower. Amazed that your mind can shape an idea, roam from Connecticut to Connemara, know yourself, a friend, God. Amazed that you can play and pray, dance and weep, like and love. Rarely bored, blasé, unfeeling – even hovering over an impacted molar or a cancerous growth. Lifeless only if you are touching merely a tooth or a lump; alive if you are in touch with a person, a man or woman or child whose ache you realise is part of them, intimate to their growing or their shrinking.

Alive, second, to your God. *Your* God. This is not pretty poetry; it is unvarnished truth. The Son of God declared that if you love him, his Father loves you, and they make their home in you (John 14:23). Amazing, isn't it? A God of eternal mystery, a God who could easily get along without you, has not only fashioned a world for you, but has chosen to live in you, to enliven you with his life, to make you more human by making you more divine. Your task together is to be *aware* of God within you, excited by his closeness, thrill to his touch.

Alive to your world, alive to your God: with such life you

can be alive to each other. I mean, ceaselessly surprised, delighted, amazed by the other. Amazed at the miracle that is your love. Amazed that your eyes could ever have met. Amazed that this first exchange should have blossomed into a lasting exchange. Amazed that in a few moments you will stand before God and the community and declare: 'All we are we give to each other, to treasure together, to share as one.' Ready to be surprised for life by the other, as a Christian is ever ready to be surprised by the Spirit. Not knowing what shape the surprise will take, knowing only that you will be surprised. All lost in wonder at the gift of God, the gift of the other.

Which leads naturally into my third point. If you are to be lost in wonder at the wonder that is the other, you have to develop a sense of the other. Rather than get lost in gossamer abstractions, let me share with you a simple, yet extraordinary, experience.

Several years ago a dear friend of mine died. Perry had been married almost 60 years. The first anniversary of his marriage he was flat broke. So he went into a florist shop, asked the florist to trust him for a single rose. The florist did; Perry brought the rose to Bess – together with a love letter. Each anniversary till he died, that lovely ritual was re-enacted: two roses, three, ten, 25, 40 – always with a love letter. And one moving afternoon in a New York restaurant, with children and grandchildren all about, before the cake was cut, in came 50 roses – with a love letter. After 50 years he still greeted his wife with an affectionate kiss after each separation, no matter how short. Wherever they walked, he offered his arm, though she needed it not. Each meal he seated her at table, even when there was no one to see. And whenever this amateur bartender (from whom I learned so much) mixed drinks for friends before dinner, no one ever drank before Perry called Bess from the kitchen – Bess who never drank – called her in for the first toast: 'To the queen!'

This is not a commercial for cocktails. That marriage lasted through good times and bad, through sickness and health, because Bess and Perry had a ceaseless sense of the other. A businessman, he never put business before Bess. A home-maker who had friends beyond counting, her priority was Perry. And together, why, the paradox was that their very concern for each other impelled them to all others – any and every person who needed their love and their care. This is how they were able to live the commandment of Jesus . . . 'This is my commandment, that you love one another as I have loved you' (John 15:12). Love one another as Jesus loved you – from a stall in Bethlehem to a cross on Calvary.

A final word, good friends. A word to all of you. You are not just an audience, spectators at a spectacle, spellbound at a sacred ceremony that involves only [bride and groom]. You are intimate to their life together, incredibly important. Married life, you know, is not lived on a fantasy island, in idyllic isolation. It calls for a community, men and women who, for all their very human differences, cherish much the same ideals. It will not be easy for [this couple] to sustain their sense of humour, their sense of wonder, their sense of the other, if their closest friends, especially their wedded friends, are humourless, wonderless, self-centred.

That is why, when [they] join hands and hearts and voices in total self-giving, I shall ask the wedded among you to link your own hands. I ask you to renew silently your own wedding vows. Not a prosaic fidelity; rather, a fresh, imaginative promise on three levels. You will try, first, to recapture a laughter you may have lost, your ability to look at yourself and your world with humour, with a loving wit. You will try, second, to recover a sense of wonder at the miracle of being alive: alive to the people around you, alive to the God within you, alive to the love tingling in the hand you hold. You will try, third, to revive your sense of the other, a ceaseless awareness of one who shares your life as no other can, as no other will.

Do that, promise that, and your gift to [this couple] will prove more precious than silver, more lasting than Irish linen. For you will share with them what is most dear to you, most private and personal and profound. You will share not only your individual love; you will share with them the love you share with each other. No greater gift can you give this day.

Walter J. Burghardt, S. J.
Grace on Crutches: Homilies for Fellow Travellers

Fourth Sunday of Epiphany
Ordinary Time 4

Mark 1:21-28

The teaching of Jesus was a teaching of life through life.

Jesus did not live up to his teaching: he lived it. There is no sign of effort or strain in what we know of his teaching, or of his life as a teacher. Effort and strain had been in the past before his teaching began.

Jesus the teacher is far more than the angelic doctor of lovely precepts conceived in the nineteenth century. Jesus discovered and taught a final wisdom; and this wisdom was such that it could be declared only by being lived. Therefore it can be learned from him only as a person. . . . We have to know the loneliness, the courage, the human perfection of the man, in order to approach the living reality of what he taught. For the teaching of Jesus was a teaching of life through life.

Jesus' teaching is, and is eternal because it is, a teaching of life. Whether Jesus himself spoke, or the author of the fourth Gospel imagined them, the secret of Jesus' teaching is in the words: 'I came that ye might have life, and have it more abundantly.' The teaching of Jesus is a joyful teaching, as all teaching of life must be, good news, indeed: a promise of infinite riches: 'Seek ye first the kingdom of heaven and all these things shall be added unto you.'

J. Middleton Murray
The Life of Jesus (abridged and slightly adapted)

Because I got very tired of being chased around a barrack square in the East Yorkshire Regiment, I volunteered to join the Royal Military Police.

In those far off days (1952), the Military Police was formed by taking two men from nearly every regiment of the British Army, giving them eighteen weeks of basic training and then sending them out to act as Army police and learn to do it the hard way: by actually being on the beat.

The 'Redcaps' as they were known were often feared and

always respected, partly I feel now as I look back because each M.P. had the authority of the Crown behind him. King's Regulations (or Queen's, if the head of State was Queen) were meant to be obeyed without question, and in my experience always were.

Sometimes the mere sight of my uniform made any private soldier replace his beret, fasten any loose button on his battledress and walk smartly on his business. Authority to maintain discipline was fine on most occasions, but sometimes it could be, and sometimes was, abused.

To this day I vividly remember a police lance-corporal in North Africa receiving a 'Dear John' letter from his girlfriend. He immediately went out, got quite drunk and arrested fifty-six squaddies on trumped-up charges.

On returning to camp he squeezed himself between the mattress and cover of his bed to sleep off his hangover, and when he woke up we had to cut him out, so tightly was he wrapped.

In Mark's Gospel, the chief priests, teachers of the law and elders recognise Jesus as being a man of authority (Mark 11:27-28). They also ask the question, 'Who gave you authority to do the things you do?' after, in the same chapter, he had 'cleansed the Temple' by driving out all the traders buying and selling there.

Significantly a Roman army officer whose servant was ill recognises that Jesus has authority to heal him, and says to Jesus, 'Just give the order and my servant will be healed'. And of course the Gospels say of Jesus that, 'He taught them as one who had authority', and that he said, after forgiving a paralysed man his sins and being criticised for it, 'You must know that the Son of Man has the authority on earth to forgive sins' (Matthew 9:6). The big question in the minds of many was: 'Does this man's authority come from God or the Evil One?'

In that the authority of Jesus always proved beneficial to people in all kinds of need, there can be only one source of that authority for me: God himself revealed as a holy, heavenly Father; deeply committed to the saving welfare of all people.

Ron Dale

Jesus leads people to learn about the unfamiliar world of the spirit from what they may see around them in the familiar world of home and field. He had the seeing eye and the hearing ear which he bade us have. In the parables he is saying to us, 'Look!' He does not argue, rather he helps us to see.

How much he saw – he bids us to look at sunrise and sunset, the ways of wind and weather. The scarlet anemone, that carpets Galilee in the springtime, was to him more splendid than a king in royal robes. He saw the weeds in the wheat fields; he was familiar with the ways of the eagle and the dove and the raven. He watched the hen gathering her chickens, the fledgling sparrow falling from the nest. He had an eye for the sheep, the ass, the dog, the camel, the wolf, the serpent, the moth. His searching glance falls too on the life of man. He knew his own trade of carpentry and house building and fishing, and the cares of the shepherd and the farmer. He knew something of the patching of old clothes and the baking of bread. He watched children at play. He painted life, the real life of rich and poor, of rogues and philanthropists, and all this knowledge and insight he turned to use in the revealing of God to us.

Hugh Martin
The Parables of the Gospels

Fifth Sunday of Epiphany
Proper 1/Ordinary Time 5

Sunday between 3 and 9 February inclusive (if earlier than the Second Sunday before Lent)

Mark 1:29-39

There came a time when I wanted and I prayed and I got a whole lot of nothing I wanted.

Hollywood film star Loretta Young's attitude to prayer at sixteen going on seventeen was: you wanted, you prayed, you got. 'Well, there came a time when I wanted and I prayed and I got a whole lot of nothing I wanted.' What Loretta wanted more than anything was to play a girl in a picture to be made called *Berkeley Square* which she loved as a stage play. It was a prestige film that would bring her fame (she thought). But she was under contract to Warners, and Twentieth Century Fox were going to make the movie.

So she told herself, 'God will fix it. All I have to do is ask.' So Loretta told God that the part belonged to her.

In the end an actress called Heather Angel was given the part and poor Loretta was desolate, tearful and bewildered. She kept thinking, 'I asked. But I did not receive. Why? Why? Why?'

Three days later her studio notified her that she had been loaned out to M. G. M. to do a low budget, real nothing of a picture called *Midnight Mary*. So she prayed for understanding and to do God's will; made the picture which turned out to be a huge success; what's more, Loretta was suddenly and unexpectedly a top star. And *Berkeley Square*, in spite of Leslie Howard's magnificent acting along with Heather Angel's beautiful and charming portrayal of the girl, was a box-office flop.

Loretta Young
The Things I had to Learn

'Mamma prays as simply, constantly and confidently as she breathes. She could no more live without praying than she could if she ceased to breathe. As a result she accepts each day's problems as calmly as she does the weather, rain or shine.'

Loretta Young
The Things I had to Learn

Feeling

Here is a tale of family life. Try to see it through the eyes of the woman whom Mark excluded from the tale. Grasp how things feel from the daughter's perspective, from the perspective of Simon's wife. Put yourself in the unenviable place of the woman caught between mother and husband. Feel that conflict in her soul.

The daughter's loyalty to her mother is deep and true. It is hard to forget the sacrifices mother made in bringing up her family. After all, times were bad and life was hard for the wife of the Galilean fisherman. Once the daughter was totally dependent on the mother. But now the tables are turned. Late, late in life, the mother is now totally dependent on the daughter. Once her husband brought home the fish, but now the home economy is supported by her daughter's husband.

How can a daughter loyal to her mother's needs see her way of life, her very security threatened by a radical change in the home economy? How can a daughter but sympathise with a mother who retreats to bed in protest or confusion?

The wife's loyalty to her husband is deep and true as well. It is hard to forget the deep-felt love and tenderness which first attracted her to the young fisherman. After all, there had been many fish in the local sea. But the choice had been made and there had been, until now, little reason to regret it. Simon had supported her and her mother, too, through days when fish were plentiful and through days when fish were scarce.

How can a wife loyal to her husband's needs stand in the way when he hears and responds to the call of God? How can a wife but understand when her husband takes time out to build the kingdom of God?

Thinking

An issue of church discipline is raised by this ancient story. The issue concerns the relationship between the call to the ministry and the demands of family life. Within some denominations the call to priestly ministry is seen as involving a simultaneous call to the life of celibacy.

Had Jesus just given the matter a little more careful thought, would he perhaps never have called the married man, Simon, away from his nets and recruited him as a frontline disciple? Had Jesus just given the matter a little more careful thought, would he perhaps only have called single men to fish souls for the kingdom?

Within some denominations, a married priesthood or a married pastorate is seen as the right and proper identification with the true and real human condition. After all, it is argued, how can ministers really identify with the majority of men and women if they, too, are not fully exposed to the joys and frustrations of family life?

But denominations which encourage (and often expect) a married priesthood must also learn to recognise the growing conflicts between the demands of ministry in a changing church and the demands of family life in a changing world. Denominations which encourage (and often expect) clergy to work from home must also learn to recognise the growing conflicts between the professional expectations of the work-place and the family expectations of the home.

Leslie J. Francis
Personality Type and Scripture: Exploring Mark's Gospel

Sixth Sunday of Epiphany
Proper 2/Ordinary Time 6

Sunday between 10 and 16 February (if earlier than the Second Sunday before Lent)

Mark 1:40-45

What loving heart could feel anything other than anger at the way in which God's perfect creation is racked with pain and disfigured with disease?

Intuition

In the ancient world leprosy was as much a crippling social disease as a crippling disease of the body. The leper was a social outcast. See Jesus' reaction as he embraces the outcast and becomes an outcast himself. Now, in the place of the leper, see the outcasts in today's society, and consider how the hand of Jesus can be stretched out to embrace them.

See the anxious face of the nine-year-old in the school playground, the persistent victim of bullying. Ask how the hand of Jesus can be stretched out to restore the battered self-esteem.

See the haunted face of the adolescent trapped in growing substance dependency, avoiding the interrogation of family, friends and the law. Ask how the hand of Jesus can be stretched out to restore the lost autonomy.

See the weary face of the single parent struggling to survive on ever-decreasing benefit, unable to afford life's social pleasures. Ask how the hand of Jesus can be stretched out to restore the lost self-confidence.

See the unshaven face of the middle-aged man grappling with the loss of employment and with the recognition that he is now unlikely to be re-employable. Ask how the hand of Jesus can be stretched out to restore the loss of self-respect.

See the greying face of the ageing widow trapped within the home she can no longer properly maintain, increasingly forgotten by family and friends. Ask how the hand of Jesus can be stretched out to restore the lost peace of mind.

See Jesus embrace the outcast leper man and carry the cost of becoming a social outcast himself.

Feeling

Awake from slumber and find yourself standing in Jesus' shoes as the leper man approaches. Find your own soul torn apart by the range of emotions which plucked at Jesus' own loving heart. In the course of such a short space of time four distinct emotions emerge.

All the ancient texts of Mark are clear that Jesus was *moved* by the sight of the leper man, *moved* by his plaintive plea for help, *moved* by his humble act of kneeling. The translations of scripture which say that Jesus was moved with pity, however, do less than justice to the ancient manuscripts and to Mark's own insight into the loving heart of Jesus.

A preferred reading of the ancient manuscripts says that Jesus was moved first with anger, not with pity. What loving heart could feel anything other than anger at the way in which God's perfect creation is racked with pain and disfigured with disease?

What loving heart could confront the leper man with any emotion less than anger? Step into Jesus' shoes and share his emotion of anger for creation racked with pain and disfigured by disease.

But then the anger gives way to compassion. What loving heart could contemplate the leper man, kneeling there, trembling in hope and anticipation of life renewed and of health restored, without going out in full compassion? What loving heart would not feel compassion in such a situation? Step into Jesus' shoes and share his emotion of compassion for humanity racked by pain and disfigured by disease.

But then the compassion gives way to resolution. The leper man has been healed and Jesus must shape his ministry elsewhere. What loving heart could rest content with one act of mercy and not plan for tomorrow's ministry? With resolution Jesus pushes the man away (again the Greek verb is harsh). With resolution Jesus commands the man to silence. With resolution Jesus is intent that the law of Moses should be observed. Step into Jesus' shoes and share his emotion of resolution.

But then the resolution gives way to frustration. The rumour that Jesus has touched the leper man spreads far and wide. For some, Jesus himself was now unclean. So they banished him from their company. For some, Jesus himself was the source of all cleansing. So they sought out his company. On both accounts, Jesus could no longer go into a town openly. Step into Jesus' shoes and share his emotion of frustration. Find yourself standing in Jesus' shoes as the leper man departs.

Leslie J. Francis
Personality Type and Scripture: Exploring Mark's Gospel

Seventh Sunday of Epiphany
Proper 3/Ordinary Time 7

Sunday between 17 and 23 February inclusive (if earlier than the Second Sunday before Lent)

Mark 2:1-12

I ain't like that any more.

Forgiven no more

Clint Eastwood's 1992 Academy Award-winning film *Unforgiven* is an extraordinarily powerful and unrelenting depiction of a world where forgiveness is assumed to be impossible or, at most, ineffective. Habits of sin, and more specifically of violence, are inescapable; they cannot be unlearned. Violence is the inescapable reality that persistently tears at the fabric of people's lives until everyone is diminished, if not destroyed, by it.

Set in the 1880s, primarily in Wyoming and neighbouring states, the film's main character is William Munny. He was 'a known thief and murderer, a man of notoriously vicious and intemperate disposition' before he married his wife. But she helped reform him of drinking and wickedness. Since her death from smallpox, he has turned to working a farm in the Kansas countryside and taking care of his two small children. He seems content to live a relatively isolated life.

He is startled one day by the arrival of a stranger. He initially denies who he is to the young man, fearing that the man has come to kill him for something he did 'in the old days'. The young man, calling himself 'The Schofield Kid', has been told that Munny was 'cold as the snow, with no weak nerve, no fear'. The bounty of one thousand dollars has been offered by some prostitutes to anyone who would come to Big Whiskey, Wyoming and kill – and thus bring vengeance on – two cowboys who have attacked and severely cut one of them.

Munny tells the Kid, 'I ain't like that any more'. His wife has changed his life. The Kid tells him that if he should change his mind, he can catch up with him on the western trail. After the Kid leaves, Munny gives the offer some thought while working with his pigs. He pulls out his guns and begins practising his shooting. Ironically, Munny in a sense 'comes to himself' – like the prodigal son – in the midst of pigs; but it is his violent self that he begins to recover. As Munny struggles to recover his aim, his young children look on in disbelief. Unaware of their father's past, the little girl wonders to her brother, 'Did Pa used to kill folks?'

Munny decides to go, explaining that he needs the money to feed his kids because his pigs are dying. Before he departs, he takes some flowers over to his wife's grave. He tells his children that he will be home in a couple of weeks, and he leaves instructions about where they should go if they need assistance. But his departure is slowed by his inability to get back into the saddle with gun in hand; evidently Munny finds it more difficult to return to his violent habits than he thought. Indeed, he observes out loud that 'the horse is getting even with me for the sins of my youth'; but he also tells his children that 'your ma showed me the error of my ways'.

On his way, Munny struggles with the acknowledgement that, in some sense, there is no need for violence; he can unlearn his habits of violence and learn to live a forgiven and forgiving life. Further, he insists – to himself as much as to an old friend, a black man named Ned, who goes with him – that going on this killing is not a reversion to old habits; he is simply doing it for the money, for the sake of his children.

Just before Munny, Ned, and the Kid arrive, the madam in Big Whiskey despairs that nobody will provide vengeance for the attack. But their arrival gives the women a hopeful glimpse that 'justice' will be served. Indeed the three men enter into a shoot-out with several cowboys from the Bar-T as they seek to kill the two cowboys who have attacked the prostitute. After a few shots, it is clear that Ned's heart is not in it anymore. So Munny takes control and shoots and kills the accomplice to the attack on the prostitute. In the meantime, Ned announces that he is heading back to Kansas and promises to look in on Munny's children. And Munny promises to bring Ned his share of the bounty.

A short while later, the prostitute who has been attacked is grieved when she hears that one of her victimisers has actually been killed. The sheriff has a quite different response when he hears about the killing. He forms a posse to look for the assassins. Before they depart, however, the sheriff is notified that people from the Bar-T have caught Ned. The sheriff brings Ned to the jail for questioning and a whipping. But when Ned is caught lying about the names of his two partners, the whippings become more severe.

At daybreak, the Kid kills the other cowboy in the Bar-T's outhouse while Munny covers him. After they flee to the sound of gunshots, they find themselves in a calm setting on a mountainside. As they drink whisky together, the Kid asks

Munny if that was what it was like in the old days. Munny can't remember the old days; he was drunk most of the time. The Kid, retelling the killing of the cowboy between shots of whisky and amid tears, admits that – contrary to earlier bravado about being a 'killer' – this was the first person he had ever killed. He plaintively observes, 'It doesn't seem right. He'll never breathe again . . . all on account of pulling a trigger.' Munny's response is poignant, though delivered matter-of-factly: 'It's a hell of a thing, killing a man.' The Kid finally explains it to himself by saying, 'I guess he had it coming'. To which Munny responds, 'We all have it coming'. For Munny, there are no easy divisions between good guys and bad, between victimisers and victims. The world and human lives are far murkier than an ability to salve consciences by saying that someone or some group 'had it coming'.

As Munny and the Kid are talking, one of the prostitutes brings them the bounty. She also reports that Ned was killed by the sheriff, perhaps accidentally; further, she indicates that his body is on display in front of the saloon with a sign indicating that this is what happens to assassins. As she recalls what she heard Ned confessing about his and Munny's past, Munny begins to chug the whisky, perhaps to stiffen his resolve, perhaps to forget once again his past, perhaps to stiffen his resolve precisely by forgetting his complex past of both violence and glimpses of peaceableness.

But the Kid will not join Munny on this killing. 'I ain't like you, Will,' he tells Munny. And so he gives Munny his gun. As Munny returns to town, he throws away the now empty whisky bottle. He enters the crowded saloon, where the sheriff is congratulating the posse on its performance. Munny kills the saloon owner for decorating his saloon with Ned. As he points the rifle at several other men, the sheriff, Little Bill, tells him: 'You're William Munny, from out of Missouri, killed women and children.' To which Munny responds, 'That's right, I killed women and children. I've killed just about everything that walked or crawled at one time or another. And I'm here to kill you, Little Bill, for what you did to Ned.'

Munny then kills five men in rapid succession and wounds the sheriff; he clears the rest of the people out the back. As Munny stares over the wounded sheriff, the sheriff tells him, 'I don't deserve this. To die like this. I was building a house.' Munny responds, 'Deserve got nothing to do with this.' The sheriff defiantly asserts, 'I'll see you in hell, William Munny.'

'Yea,' Munny agrees, as he kills him. As Munny leaves town, he yells to any and all people that they had better give

Ned a proper burial, or else he'll be back and kill them all. As he rides out of town, and as the film ends, there is very little life left; the prostitutes and a few of the townspeople watch with lifeless horror.

Despite the horrifying violence in the film, it does not glorify violence the way many westerns do. It is far too morally serious for such a depiction. Rather, it suggests that human beings are filled with both the possibility of goodness and the capacity for great destruction. In this sense there is no stable *self* that can be presumed to be fundamentally good or fundamentally evil; rather, our selves are battlefields in which we can never claim complete control. Either we are constrained by the forces of sin and evil, the habits of death, or we learn to be constrained by the very practices of forgiveness and reconciliation through which God's peace is communicated.

Further, the story shows the fragility of our commitments to unlearn and break our habits of sin. If such commitments are to be sustained, they require supportive friendships, practices and institutions that enable the unlearning of destructive habits and the cultivation of holy ones. The film suggests that those friendships, practices and institutions are absent precisely because of their fragility in the face of violence and vengeance. It takes only a moment to destroy lives through violence, but it takes lifetimes to cultivate alternative patterns and practices of forgiveness, of trust, of love.

L. Gregory Jones
Embodying Forgiveness

Eighth Sunday of Epiphany
Second Sunday before Lent*
Ordinary Time 8

Mark 2:13-22

Leadership that knows where it is going is hard to come by in our society.

I was to be fifty in a year's time, and the magic of numbers asserted itself. At fifty, I thought, I must make a definite decision: either to remain where I was or to effect some sort of radical change. It was then or never. I should be too old, too completely dug in, if I put off the decision further. Would I have the nerve to make it? It occurred to me that during the whole of my life I had never taken any fundamental initiative. I had merely accepted what had been offered me on a plate – the curacies in London, the chaplaincy at Westcott House, the Fellowship at Trinity. I had not pulled even the smallest string to get any of these jobs. Wasn't I a bit old to begin making a future for myself and perhaps actually applying somewhere for a place or a job? It had never dawned on me before how protected my life had been. Hitherto I had, without realising it, assumed that things just came one's way. I had, it is true, lived my adult life in the early postwar period when there was no unemployment to speak of. But people, none the less, did choose to do this rather than that and took steps accordingly. I never had. The possible prospect of it alarmed me not a little.

The spring vacation (it was 1968) promised me some temporary relief from the choice hanging over me. I flew to Shetland for a fortnight's holiday with two of the Ramblers – Elizabeth Cavendish and John Betjeman. We based ourselves at Lerwick. The morning after our arrival we woke up to find thick snow on the ground which immobilised us for two days. We had to remain in the hotel and read, with occasional sessions in front of the television . . .

Easter Sunday came, and I thought I had better go to church, partly out of a sense of duty and partly not to upset John, for whom at that time (he is no longer like that) attendance at the Holy Communion on Sunday was a bit of a neurotic compulsion; all the more so, therefore, on Easter Sunday. So the three of us went to the small episcopal church

*See page 30 for readings related to John 1:1-14 (CWL).

in Lerwick. There were about twelve other people in the congregation at this eight o'clock service, and the priest was a youngish man attended by the usual adolescent server in his middle teens. We didn't discover to whom the church was dedicated, but for me personally it was quite definitely Trinity church, for it was there that I met my doom. The priest read the usual Prayer Book epistle for Easter Sunday, and a sentence of it burnt into me like fire: 'Ye died, and your life is hid with Christ in God.' The words overpowered me. It was like being struck fiercely in the face. Yet it wasn't like that either. For if the impact of the words was merciless, it was the impact of a merciless mercy. What pounced upon me was not so much a divine imperative as a divine invitation, though I suppose it could be said that these are different ways of saying much the same thing. Yet not always or necessarily. For what strikes somebody as a divine imperative may be a projection upon the heavens of his own pathological guilt feelings. But an invitation, however compelling, is never compulsive. It has about it a supreme graciousness which frightens only because it attracts so mightily. From that moment I knew beyond a peradventure that I was being invited to die somehow to an old life in order to find a truer identity in the encompassing mystery of which I had been so long aware. In practical terms this meant leaving Cambridge and writing to Geoffrey Beaumont about the possibility of the Mirfield Community being willing to give me a try.

H. A. Williams
Some Day I'll Find You

What can a person say? He can lift up and commend two words of Jesus that resonate with relevance for people today: 'Follow me.'

Jesus uttered these words not once but many times: to Peter and Andrew by the Sea of Galilee; to Levi, the son of Alphaeus at the seat of customs . . . to the rich young ruler: 'Sell what you have, give to the poor, and come, follow me'. And to all in his time and succeeding times, 'If any man would come after me, let him deny himself and take up his cross and follow me.'

. . . There are several considerations that have moved me in recent months to a new appreciation of these words. First, anyone who says 'Follow me' is going someplace – and we need direction. These words strike us initially as unwelcome and intrusive. They threaten to dislocate us. But ponder them longer and find that part of their appeal lies in the fact that *they promise to connect us with someone who is going someplace.*

The therapy of hibernation, so widely practised by so many in our time, cannot really heal what hurts us deep inside. Yet leadership that knows where it is going is hard to come by in our society, and so we hibernate. There was more truth than humour to the legend I spotted on a T-shirt in New Hampshire a few summers back, 'Don't follow me, I'm lost'. . . .

Jesus has a plan, a work to do, a purpose to achieve in history and beyond. And he deigns to cut us in. The word that is translated *follow* in most instances in the Gospel is rooted in the Greek word for *road*. To follow is to share the same road. The Christian's prayer is not for a longer stay with God but for a closer walk with God. Moreover, anyone who says 'Follow me' is obviously more interested in the future than in the past – and we need a loyalty to the future. With Jesus it's not where you've been that matters, but where you're going; not whether you have fallen, but whether you will get up; not whom you've hurt in the past, but whom you will help in the future.

Ernest T. Campbell
From a sermon called *Follow me*

Ninth Sunday of Epiphany

Mark 2:23-3:6

Intuition

If you could re-write Sundays the way you would want them to be, where would you draw the line?

The Pharisees were running a campaign to keep the Sabbath special. Jesus fell foul of the way they thought the Sabbath should really be kept. Their campaign to keep the Sabbath special required people to desist from plucking corn. Their campaign to keep the Sabbath special required people to desist from non-emergency healings.

Now, if you could re-write Sundays the way you would want them to be, where would you draw the line? What provision would you like there to be? Would you keep the hospitals running just like any other day of the week, to get the best return from expensive equipment and highly developed operating theatres? Or would you try and assign a rest day to a higher proportion of the staff?

If you could re-write Sundays, would you keep the petrol station open to refuel your car? Would you keep the corner shop open to purchase your paper and the extra pint of milk? Or would you want the staff of these places to benefit from an extra day at home?

If you could re-write Sundays, would you open the supermarket, the garden centre and the home improvement store, so that much of the day-to-day business could go on undisturbed? Or would you want to signal that such activities are disruptive of family life and of religious sensitivities?

If you could re-write Sundays, would you see an opportunity for major sporting fixtures, to take the pressure off Saturday and to provide families with something to do? Or would you want to make sure that the churches were operating in a less competitive market place?

Now, if you could re-write Sundays the way you would want them to be, where would you draw the line? What provision would you like there to be?

Feeling

Now see how the whole thing looks to the man with the withered hand.

It must have all seemed so strange to the man with the withered hand. The hand had been like that for years. It had been like that on weekdays; it had been like that on Sabbaths. But never before had the withered hand caused so much controversy.

Year in and year out he had longed to come face to face with a real healer who could have made that hand as good as new. But never before had he seen a real healer in that town.

Sabbath by Sabbath he had been to that synagogue and no one had as much as noticed that he was there. But today he had been the centre of all attention. The Pharisees and Scribes had fixed their eyes on him from the moment he walked in through the open door. Then Jesus had called him to step forward.

He stood there on the very edge of being healed, waiting with excitement and expectation. But instead of being the centre of miraculous healing, he stood at the heart of theological controversy.

All he heard was a simple command, 'Stretch out your hand'. All he did was to obey the command. He stretched out his hand and it was restored.

As he returned home healed and restored, he heard the whispering conspiracy of the Pharisees. They were plotting to kill the man who had healed him.

Leslie J. Francis
Personality Type and Scripture: Exploring Mark's Gospel

Last Sunday of Epiphany
Sunday next before Lent
Transfiguration Sunday

Mark 9:2-9

*Just occasionally
in our spiritual
life the curtains of
heaven are pulled
back and we are
vouchsafed a vision
of the glorious
reality of God.*

Sight, light, illumination are constant metaphors of grace: and the metaphor itself is many-sided. For first, we are in the dark about God, and the whole world of things acts as a screen of darkness we cannot penetrate, and God is above, behind, within. But then second, we are in the dark about the world, for we can see none of it as it is, and especially we can see no fellow-humans as they are until we learn to see them through the eyes of God. Third, we are in the dark about our way, not knowing what path to follow, like wanderers in a jungle; for only the sheer shining of God's will can tell us what is our calling in life; and what tracks are to be shunned, what explored. But fourth, we are in the dark, a sad darkness has invaded us and settled upon us; for we do not know what it is to live in the light, until we are turned to God and engaged in doing his will for the love of him. Then the worldly world, and our own will and eyes, shine with a beautiful clearness which is the climate of heaven. In all these ways the grace of God is light.

Austin Farrer
Words for Life

Sensing

The transfiguration is a narrative rich in sensory images. So come and explore.

Put on your climbing shoes and come climbing. Climb, climb, climb the high mountain. Feel the atmosphere change as you rise high above the pollution. Hear the sounds of traffic, chatter and work grow faint as you rise high above the noise. See the sights of people, houses and farms grow small, as you rise high above the world. Standing there, high on the mountain, you feel on top of the world and as if you have

81

approached the gateway to heaven. Put on your climbing shoes and come climbing.

Put on your glasses and come looking. Look, look, look carefully as Jesus stands there before you. See Jesus transfigured before your very eyes. See Jesus' clothes become dazzling white, whiter than any washing powder's wildest dream. See the sky open and Elijah and Moses appear. Standing there surrounded by such powerful sights, you feel as if you have approached the gateway to heaven. Put on your glasses and come looking.

Plug in your personal stereo and come listening. Listen, listen, listen carefully as Jesus stands there before you. Hear the divine voice speak from the clouds. Hear the affirmation and hear the command. 'This is my Son, the Beloved; listen to him!' Standing there surrounded by such powerful sounds you feel as if you have approached the gateway to heaven. Plug in your personal stereo and come listening.

The transfiguration is a narrative rich in sensory images. So come and explore.

Intuition

Just occasionally in our spiritual life the curtains of heaven are pulled back and we are vouchsafed a vision of the glorious reality of God. I wonder what your experience has been?

Have you been out climbing and risen high above the mundane issues of daily life? Has the majesty of height opened your heart to the presence of God?

Have you been out walking at night when the sky is clear and when the stars shine bright? Has the magnitude of the night sky opened your heart to the presence of God?

Have you been out sailing on the still and open sea miles from all sight of land? Has the vastness of the waters opened your heart to the presence of God?

Have you been out visiting some prehistoric site where the forces of nature have shaped the landscape? Has the unrecorded passing of time opened your heart to the presence of God?

Have you been out looking into the face of a newborn child and recognised the archetype of humanity? Has the mystery of human life opened your heart to the presence of God?

Have you been out worshipping in the midst of the people

of God where the Spirit is at work? Has the conviction of the Spirit's activity opened your heart to the presence of God?

Have you been out meditating alone before the blessed sacrament? Has the reality of the body of Christ opened your heart to the presence of God?

Just occasionally in our spiritual life the curtains of heaven are pulled back and we are vouchsafed a vision of the glorious reality of God. I wonder what your experiences have been?

Thinking

If we are going to appreciate the theological significance of Mark's account of the transfiguration, we must begin to interrogate some of his detail.

Why, so uncharacteristically, does Mark begin the narrative with such a precise location in time? Why *six days later*? Was this simply to bind this narrative to Peter's confession at Caesarea Philippi? Or is this a deliberate echo of the six days during which Moses waited before the Lord spoke out of a cloud (Exodus 24)?

Why does Mark locate the narrative so precisely *up a high mountain*? Was this simply to emphasise encounter with transcendence? Or is there a deliberate echo of God's decisive revelation to the people of the old Israel on Mount Sinai? (Exodus 24).

Why does Mark describe with such care the *dazzling* whiteness of Jesus' clothes? Was this simply to emphasise the supernatural nature of the occurrence? Or is there a deliberate echo of the way in which Moses had been transfigured by his encounter with God on the mountain? (Exodus 34).

Why does Mark identify so clearly the presence of Elijah and Moses? Was this simply to emphasise continuity with the old order? Or is there a deliberate allusion to Jesus being affirmed by the Law and the Prophet? And had not Malachi (chapter 4) promised that Elijah would come before the great and terrible day of the Lord?

Why does Mark refer so purposefully to the voice coming from the cloud? Was this simply to emphasise the mysterious nature of the revelation? Or is there a deliberate attempt to identify the voice as that of God alone, who spoke to Moses out of the self same cloud? (Exodus 24).

Why does Mark attribute to the divine voice words both

so similar and so dissimilar to those cited at the moment of baptism? Is this carelessness or deliberate subtlety? At the baptism, when Jesus was anointed Messiah by the baptiser, God spoke to Jesus and to Jesus alone, 'You are my Son, the Beloved'. At the transfiguration, when Jesus' anointed Messiahship had been recognised and confessed by Peter, God spoke publicly, 'This is my Son, the Beloved'.

If we are going to appreciate the theological significance of Mark's account of the transfiguration, we must begin to interrogate some of this detail.

Leslie J. Francis
Personality Type and Scripture: Exploring Mark's Gospel

First Sunday of Lent
(see also under the Baptism of the Lord, p. 51)

Mark 1:9-15

A son of God is not someone who is related to God by rising out of his humanity, but someone who is beloved by God for sinking into it even when he is famished, even when he is taunted by the devil himself.

I sat in the desert once myself, just to see what it was like. The first thing I noticed was how quiet it was, so quiet that I could hear the racket that my body makes – gurgle, wheeze, thump. Did you know that if you can get quiet enough, you can actually hear the hum of your own electricity? It makes about as much noise as the motor on a small electric clock, only most of us cannot hear it because of all the other motors around us. In the desert, you can.

The second thing I noticed was how fast I got lonely. There is something about a desert that can suck all the self-confidence right out of you. It is so big, so quiet, so empty that you cannot help noticing how small and perishable you are. You remember that you are dust and to dust you shall return. You wish you had someone to distract you from that fact, or at least someone to talk to about it. Anyone but the devil, that is.

The third thing I noticed was the flies, but based on my own experience, I feel certain that if they did not constitute a fourth temptation for Jesus then they at least made the other three harder to bear, because nothing can try your spirit like a fly. There I was in the desert, trying to commune with Jesus, and all I could think of was that fly – circling my head, buzzing in my ears, trying to crawl up my nose. Flies are perfect tools of the devil: so you think you're pretty spiritual, huh? Well, try one of these for size . . .

I cannot help thinking that something like that was going on with Jesus in the wilderness. Remember that he had just come from his own baptism, where everyone present had seen the sky break open, watched the dove descend and heard the voice from heaven introduce God's own Son. After something like that, everyone, including Jesus, might have expected him to sprout wings and fly away. They might have looked for him to become a kind of super hero, who would cease being human in order to rescue human beings, showing up in the nick of time to snatch them out of danger.

Only that was not what happened. What happened was that he went from one spectacular moment to a long, lonely time in the wilderness, during which he may have wondered if he had imagined the whole thing. For forty days and forty nights there was no sign of God at all. The sky stayed shut.

There were no doves. No voice from heaven spoke reassuring words. There was just him, the desert, and finally, the devil . . .

All along, the devil subtly suggested that Jesus deserved better than God was giving him. Why should the Son of God be famished? Why should he so much as stub his toe, or be subject to Caesar when Caesar should be subject to him? If God could do no better than that by his Son, the devil suggested, maybe Jesus should start shopping around for another father.

This is the story in which everyone finds out what being the Son of God really means. This is the story in which Jesus proves who he is not by seizing power, but turning it down. God's Beloved will not practise magic. He will not ask for special protection or seek political power. But as much as it may surprise everyone, including him, he will remain human, accepting all the usual risks.

It is, after all, the only way in which humans will ever learn what 'Son of God' really means. A son of God is not someone who is related to God by rising out of his humanity, but someone who is beloved by God for sinking into it even when he is famished, even when he is taunted by the devil himself. It is someone who can listen to every good reason in the world for becoming God's rival and remain God's child instead.

This is chiefly a story about Jesus' identity, but insofar as we belong to him, it is a story about our identity, too. There are plenty of times when we too are tempted to believe that we deserve bigger and better than what we have. That devilish voice in our head says things like, 'If you are a child of God, shouldn't things be going a little smoother for you? If you are really a Christian, I mean – shouldn't you be happier, healthier, richer, safer?'

You know what to say back now, right? 'Away with you, Satan! I would rather be a hungry child of God that a well-fed player on your team. Now shoo!'

If you can manage that, then the chances are very good that you will hear another voice in your head before long, ten thousand times more beautiful than the first. 'This is my beloved child,' the voice will say, 'in whom I am well pleased.'

Barbara Brown Taylor
Bread of Angels

Barbara Brown Taylor holds the Harry R. Butman Chair in Religion and Philosophy at Piedmont College in Demorest, Georgia. On a recent Newsweek television programme Barbara was described as one of the top twelve preachers and broadcasters in America today.

Second Sunday in Lent

Mark 8:31-38 or 9:2-9*

Let us never allow the pious, churchy, conventional use of the cross as an ornament, smothered in gold, silver, brass, flowers, to hide the original, stark, revolting deed.

'. . . We preach Christ crucified, a stumbling block to Jews and folly to Gentiles . . .' (1 Corinthians 1:23 RSV).

'. . . The stumbling-block of the cross has been removed' (Galatians 5:11b RSV).

Not many initially may suspect a connection between a mousetrap and the cross of Christ! Yet it is here in this very phrase, for the Greek word is *skandalon* which is a wire pin as the trigger of a trap which, after the bait has lured to a nibble, suddenly snaps and takes the victim unawares! The sensation is unpleasant, a surprise, a shock. It is like treading on a long-handled rake or brush in the dark which gets up and hits us suddenly. It upsets, it scandalises.

In the Old Testament (Isaiah 8:13-16) it foretells that the Lord of Hosts will become a rock of stumbling and a stone of offence to both houses of Israel, a trap and a snare . . . and many shall stumble thereon; they shall fall and be broken, snared and taken. Scandal is a term used quite frequently in the New Testament, and today in the popular press and in general conversation. Jesus said, 'Blessed is he who takes no offence at me' (Matthew 11:6).

Sometimes it is translated *stumbling-block*, like tripping over an unseen obstacle. We are pulled up sharp and make a wry face like Tom in *The Water Babies* when fed with pebbles instead of sweets. This is the offence, something that puts us off and tends to create misgiving. Jesus recognised the element in himself. His own townsmen observed, 'Is not this the carpenter's son?' The Pharisees saw he was friendly with disreputable people and sat lightly to traditional conventions. Whenever the shadow of the cross fell across the scene his disciples shivered. He warned his own disciples, telling them so that they should not be scandalised (John 16:1).

This upsetting, offensive, off-putting, scandalous element was concentrated in the cross of Christ, which focused the whole matter to one, hard, bright point. The apostles afterwards recognised this inescapable factor, to the good people

*For readings related to Mark 9:2-9, see page 81

scandalous, to the clever and artistic people ridiculous and repulsive.

So let us never allow the pious, churchy, conventional use of the cross as an ornament, smothered in gold, silver, brass, flowers, to hide the original, stark, revolting deed.

It is a horrible to see a man, especially a good man, nailed on a cross to prevent him being able to grip and control himself, exposed like a scarecrow, helplessly hanging with blood, sweat and tears pouring from him. Crucifixion is the most humiliating and contemptible form of execution, reserved for criminals, slaves and vermin, associated with shame and shock for ever. The whole process is deliberately off-putting.

Imagine yourself present. In any group or from any point of view it is loathsome, repulsive, shocking, scandalous. Its purpose was to stifle the influence of Christ from the start. His enemies, political, legal, moral, religious, jeered. The masses were stupefied, his lieutenants shaken to the core. The incarnation of all their hopes was pinned to the supreme symbol of humiliated defeat. It was as if they had trodden on a long-handled rake in the dark. The trap had clamped down with a bang and a crack. The followers were caught in a corner like sheep for the slaughter. The rest presumably put off for ever!

No wonder hostile critics then (as now) were not slow to point out, amidst the embarrassing publicity of the whole affair, the apparent futility of the occasion. The claims of Jesus and his followers had made shipwreck at the cross. Here was the greatest challenge to show any effective meaning except one more major and final disillusionment. This stumbling-block is the chief task of the disciples to remove if they can. Actually Christian theology was irritated into existence by this effort to explain the death of Jesus.

Rev. T. D. Meadley
Unpublished sermon

Former principal of Cliff College, methodist minister, scholar and preacher, deceased.

Among the Jews at the time of Jesus the cross was known as the *tau*, the last letter of the Hebrew alphabet, which formerly was written as a standing or an oblique cross with corresponding letters in the Greek and Latin alphabet. This *tau* had a special significance. It functioned as a symbol of belonging to God, as a sign of penitence and protection . . .

This probably was also the way in which Jesus and the Jewish Christians first understood the cross: as a seal and symbol of belonging and protection.

Those who follow Jesus, be they children, women or men, must bear the tau on their foreheads. They no longer belong to themselves. They are Christ's, stand under his protection and thus receive a new identity. Later, in baptism, the cross sign was in fact made upon those who joined the company of Christ.

. . . But they did not separate the event of Golgotha from the subsequent resurrection of their Lord. For them the cross was never the sign of a sad memory, but always a reminder of their crucified and risen Lord. What Jews and Jewish Christians understood essentially as a symbol of belonging and protection has for gentile Christians and the ancient church become a symbol of victory and triumph. From the fourth century onwards, therefore, the cross is often adorned with precious stones . . .

At first sight the reality of the crucifixion totally contradicts the cross as a symbol of triumph and transfiguration. It was so horrible that the highly educated Roman orator said in his defence of Senator C. Rabirius: 'Should death be threatening, then we want to die in freedom. The executioner, the covering of the head and the mere mention of the word *cross* must all be banned not only from the body and life of Roman citizens, but also from their thoughts, ears and eyes.'

Hans-Reudi Weber
On a Friday Noon

Third Sunday of Lent

John 2:13-22

Disillusionment is the loss of illusion – about ourselves, about the world, about God – and while it is almost always painful, it is not a bad thing . . . disillusioned, we come to understand that God does not conform to our expectations.

The following extended passage speaks of the death of the Christian Church in Turkey; the death of faith; the rise of disillusionment; but ends on a note of hope for the re-building of faith in God and his Church, as building and Body of Christ.

Two summers ago, I travelled to north-eastern Turkey for a walk in the Kachkar Mountains, a stretch of land between the Black and Caspian seas where the kingdom of Georgia flourished during the eleventh and twelfth centuries. During its brief ascendance in this part of the world, Georgia was a kind of Camelot, a Christian kingdom in which strong and benevolent rulers carved a culture out of the wilderness and defended it from its enemies. They imported Byzantine artists from Constantinople to adorn their public buildings, and built an economy that prospered all their subjects. Two hundred years later it was all gone, torn to pieces by neighbouring tribes. Now it is a wilderness again, although a beautiful one – a kingdom of mountains, tall pines, and rushing streams populated only by the handful of people who have found flat places to farm.

One afternoon in the middle of nowhere, a guide led a group of trekkers up a dirt road toward a small settlement hidden behind some trees. We turned a bend and the outline of a ruined cathedral appeared, a huge grey stone church with a central dome that dominated the countryside. Grass grew between what was left of the roof tiles and the façade was crumbling, but even in shambles, it spoke to us. The whole group fell silent before it, looking around for permission to enter, but no permission was necessary. It was a hull, a shell. No living thing remained inside, and we were free to explore.

Arriving at the main portal, I stepped through and was swallowed up by the sheer size of the space inside. Very little of the roof had survived, but the massive walls still held plaster frescoes with the shadows of biblical scenes on them. There were lambs of God carved on the stone capitals and medieval saints with their faces chipped away. Some of the best stones had been plundered for other purposes, but those that remained testified to the care and expense that had been lavished on this house of God.

Poking around, I found evidence of camp fires in one side chapel. The other had been turned into a garbage dump, where rats prowled for scraps. From the transept I heard the sound of children playing soccer on the floor of the central nave, while a couple of sheep grazed under the apse. In the dome just above it was still possible to see one outstretched arm of the Pantocrator who had presided over the Eucharist; the rest of him had flaked away. Sitting down under what was left of his embrace, I surveyed the ruins of his church.

It is one thing to talk about the post-Christian era and quite another to walk around inside it. Christianity died in Turkey – the land that gave birth to Paul and that he found so fertile for the sowing of his Gospel – the land of Ephesus, Galatia, Colossae, Nicea. Today the Christian population of Turkey is less than one percent of the total. Churches that were the jewels of Byzantine Christendom have been stripped of their altars, fonts and crosses. Many have been turned into mosques while others are open to tourists as museums and still others have been left to rot. Looking round that magnificent Georgian cathedral that had been abandoned for almost a thousand years, I imagined my own parish in its place: the beautiful wooden rafters rotted out and the ceiling collapsed, shards of stained glass hanging from the window panes, the carved stone altar removed to some museum along with the processional cross – vestiges of an ancient faith no longer practised in the land. Such a thing is not impossible.

Such a thing is not impossible; that is what I learned in that ruin on the hillside. God has given us good news in human form and has even given us the grace to proclaim it, but part of our terrible freedom is the freedom to lose our voices, to forget where we were going and why. While that knowledge does not yet strike me as prophetic, it does keep me from taking both my own ministry and the ministry of the whole church for granted. If we do not attend to God's presence in our midst and bring all our best gifts to serving that presence in the world, we may find ourselves selling tickets to a museum.

As best I can figure, the Christian era ended during my lifetime. When I was eight years old in small-town Alabama, there was nothing to do on Sundays but to go to church . . .

By the time I reached high school, God was dead. Pictures of Kent State and the My Lai massacres were tattooed on people's minds, and they turned their outrage on what they had been taught about God. God was not good. God did not answer prayer. God, for all practical purposes, was dead. All bets were off. Human beings were free to construct their own realities from any materials at hand and to express themselves any way they pleased. When lightning did not strike, their confidence grew along with their fear: that perhaps they really were alone in the universe after all.

Organised religion remained one of the many choices available to human beings in their search for meaning, but it was a lame one. On the college campus where I spent the early seventies, my peers let me know that only the unimaginative still went to church – the stuck, the fearful, the socially inept – while those with any sense committed themselves to more relevant causes, like the anti-war movement, or the environment, or the arts. Church-like communities formed around such causes, giving their members identity, purpose and support. They had their own ideologies and codes of behaviour as rigid as those of any religion, but no one seemed to notice. We gave our allegiance freely; it was not required of us, and whom we gave it to was each other.

That was almost twenty years ago, and the trend has continued. Faith in God is no longer the rule; it is the exception to the rule, one 'option' among many for people seeking to make sense out of their lives. A large number of them have been so wounded by their religious training that belief in God is too painful to consider. Not long ago I heard a mother defend her grown-up daughter's ignorance of Christianity. She herself had been schooled in a French Canadian convent, where nuns had bullied her for years in the name of God. When she escaped them, she vowed to protect her own children. 'My daughter doesn't know Moses from Goliath,' she says with some pride, 'but at least she grew up without guilt.'

Others feel betrayed by a God whom they believe to have broken an implicit promise. According to their Sunday school teachers, God made a bargain with each one of them the moment they were born: do what I say and I will take care of you. So they did, and for years it seemed to work. They obeyed their parents, their teachers, their coaches and they were taken care of, but one day the system failed. They did everything right and everything went wrong. Their prayers went unanswered, their belief went unrewarded, their God went AWOL, and the lie was exposed. One man I know, mourning the death of his infant daughter, confessed the depth of his loss. 'I don't know what to believe any more,' he said. 'I don't know who to pray to, or what to pray. I tried to be a good person; I did the best I knew how, and it didn't do a bit of good. If God is going to let something like this happen, then what's the use of believing at all?'

His disillusionment is emblematic of the post-Christian era, when the perceived promises of Christendom lie broken and the existence of God – never mind the omnipotence of

God – seems a fantasy. Television evangelists are indicted for fraud and parish priests for child molestation; churches pour their resources into institutional survival while their members dwindle; religious wars are waged around the world while children's bellies bloat and whole species disappear off the face of the earth. These are grim times, in which the God of our fondest dreams is nowhere to be found.

But down in the darkness below those dreams – in the place where all our notions about God have come to naught – there is still reason to hope. Because disillusionment is not so bad. Disillusionment is the loss of illusion – about ourselves, about the world, about God – and while it is almost always painful, it is not a bad thing to lose the lies we have mistaken for the truth. Disillusioned, we come to understand that God does not conform to our expectations. We glimpse our own relative size in the universe and see that no human being can say who God should be or how God should act. We review our requirements of God and recognise them as our own fictions, our own frail shelters against the vast night sky. Disillusioned, we find out what is not true and are set free to seek what is – if we dare.

Many of the disillusioned do not have the heart to pursue such freedom. The pain of their loss is too great. They have been robbed of the God who was supposed to be, and their fear of the God who might be makes it impossible for them to move. Anger becomes their best defence – anger at the hardness of their lives, and at those who led them to expect more, anger at their own gullibility. Some are able to use their anger as a bridge back to God, but many more set their bridges on fire, denying the presence of God with all the fury of a rejected lover.

But there are also people who have let the idea of God go as easily as an old pair of shoes. They seem to be people who never expected much in the first place, who are so used to being let down by parents, by friends, by life – that discarding their hopes comes as naturally to them as breathing. They learned early on that belief is nothing but a shortcut to disappointment, so they saved themselves the trouble, retiring belief in God with belief in Santa Claus, Lady Luck and the Tooth Fairy.

. . . Did God fail to come when I called? Did God fail to punish my adversary? Then perhaps God is not a policeman. So who is God? Did God fail to make everything turn out all right? Then perhaps God is not a fixer. So who is God? . . .

It is the question of a lifetime, and the answers are never big enough or finished. Pushing past curtain after curtain, it becomes clear that the failure is not God's but my own, for having such a poor and stingy imagination. God is greater than my imagination, wiser than my wisdom, more dazzling than the universe, as present as the air I breathe and utterly beyond my control. That is, in short, what makes me a Christian. As the creature of a God like that, I need a mediator, an advocate, a flesh-and-blood handle on the inscrutable mystery that gives birth to everything that is. While Jesus is, in his own way, just as inscrutable, he is enough like me to convince me that relationship with God is not only possible, but deeply desired by God, who wants me to believe that love is the wide net spread beneath the most dangerous of my days.

To believe that is an act of faith – not a one-time decision, but a daily, sometimes hourly, choice to act as if that were true in spite of all the evidence to the contrary. Sometimes it feels like pure make-believe. I read the weekend newspaper, full of stories about violence, addiction, corruption, disaster and I wonder whom I am kidding. Or my own life begins to spring leaks and I lie awake in the middle of the night faint with fear. I want a safer world. I want a more competent God. Then I remember that God's power is not a controlling but a redeeming power – the power to raise the dead, including those who are destroying themselves – and the red blood of belief begins to return to my veins . . . I am in good hands; love girds the universe; God will have the last word.

That, it seems to me, is where we are at the edge of the twenty-first century – 'we' being the Church of God, the Body of Christ on earth. In this age of a million choices, we are the remnant, the sometimes faithful, sometimes unfaithful family of a difficult and glorious God, called to seek and proclaim God's presence in a disillusioned world. It is a world that claims to have left us behind, along with dragons and a flat earth, but meanwhile the human heart continues to hunt its true home. Today it is crystals and past-life readings; tomorrow it may be travel to Mars. Ours is a restless and impatient race, known for abandoning our saviours as quickly as we elect them for not saving us soon or well or often enough.

. . . Our job is to stand with one foot on earth and one in heaven, with the double vision that is the gift of faith, and to say out of our own experience that reality is not flat but deep, not opaque but transparent, not meaningless but shot full of grace for those with the least willingness to believe it to be so.

Barbara Brown Taylor
The Preaching Life

Fourth Sunday of Lent

John 3:14-21

To love what was broken, torn, peeling. . . To love what smelled and what nobody else would scrape away the filth of to identify. . . To love and to hold on to it.

Billy Bathgate is the story of a young boy growing up in the Depression in America. The book's cover describes him as a 'capable boy' who 'tells his own tale of fateful adventures in pages peopled with such personalities as Abbadabba Berman who invents a way to change the day's winning number at the last minute; the fastidious Irving who mixes drinks with the same precision as he disposes of dead men; the lovely Miss Lola Miss Drew, (sic) who dresses herself in cream and aqua to run away with the killer of her dreams and the one-time Bronx kid Arthur Flegenheimer, known by the world as Dutch Schulz. . . It is a richly detailed report of a fifteen-year-old boy's journey from childhood to adulthood . . . Billy Bathgate is kind-hearted, sharp-witted, original, likeable and always completely believable. He's Huck Finn and Tom Sawyer with more poetry . . .

Billy grows up in an orphanage and one day he describes how: 'I had long ceased to play there, having taken to wandering down the hill to the other side of Webster Avenue, where there were gangs of boys my own age. . . . But I still liked to keep in touch with one or two of the incorrigible girls, and I still liked to visit Arnold Garbage. I don't know what his real name was but what did it matter? Every day of his life he wandered through the Bronx and lifted the lids of ashcans and found things. He poked about in the streets and down the alleys and in the front halls under the stairs and in the empty lots and in the backyards and behind the stores and in the basements. It was not easy work because in those days of our life trash was a commodity and there was competition for it. Junk-men patrolled with their two-wheeled carts, and the peddlers with their packs, and organ grinders and hobos and drunks, but also people who weren't particularly looking for scavenge until they saw it. But Garbage was genius, he found things that other junkers discarded, he saw value in stuff the lowest, most down-and-out and desperate street bum wouldn't touch. He had some sort of innate mapping facility, different days of the month attracted him to different neighbourhoods, and I think his mere presence on a street was enough to cause people to start flinging things down the stairs and out the windows. And his years of collecting had accustomed everyone to respect it; he never went to school, he never did his chores, he lived as if he were alone and it all worked beautifully for this fat, intelligent, almost speechless boy who had found this way to live with such mysterious single-minded and insane purpose that it seemed natural and logical and you wondered why you didn't live that way yourself. To love what was broken, torn, peeling. To love what didn't work. To love what was twisted and cracked and missing its parts. To love what smelled and what nobody else would scrape away the filth of to identify. To love what was indistinct in shape and indecipherable in purpose and indeterminate in function. To love and to hold on to it.

E. L. Doctorrow
Billy Bathgate

Submission to the 'lifting up' on the Cross is as much a divine commandment for the saving of the world as Moses' act in 'lifting up' the serpent was for the healing of the people. It is in itself not only an act of Christ, but an act of God. There is complete agreement of will between Christ and the Father. Thus John 3:16 is not merely a theological reflection of the Evangelist, but a statement of the Christian Gospel of the Cross. It describes a heavenly 'mystery' which the Son of Man discloses in word and act. The Evangelist further interprets the Cross as judgement. Christ is thus lifted up, and shares the divine throne. The Judgement Day is now, and not only in the future. The immediate purpose of Jesus' coming is not to 'judge' humanity, i.e. to pass sentence on them, but to save them, which is an exact interpretation of Jesus' mission to the publicans and sinners. Yet rejection of him inevitably judges. Just as a person is judged by their ignorant opinion of a great picture, or adverse criticism of a good individual's work or character, so people are judged by their attitude towards Jesus, and in particular towards the love revealed in the Cross. The primary purpose of the sun is not to cast shadows, but it does.

Here and now, unbelief in Christ involves condemnation. If the word 'judgement' sounds harsh we must remember that the environment in which [these words] are spoken is one where the acceptance or rejection of the Christian message did indicate a dividing line between good and evil, right and wrong ways of living. There was then no civilisation unconsciously permeated by Christian standards. The Christian way of life, based on whole-hearted belief in Christ, was distinct from the pagan way. It was a moment in the history of the world when the Church saw clearly that on belief in and obedience to Jesus Christ, the fate of the world depended. Is it not demanded of us that we think of the future of civilisation in the same clear terms today?

R. H. Strachan, D. D.
The Fourth Gospel: Its Significance and Environment

Fifth Sunday of Lent

John 12:20-33

*Now comes
my hour of
heartbreak.*

Here is a true story from the old American West that reveals some of the problems of sowing for a harvest, both physical and spiritual!

In the San Juan pueblo, almost three hundred years after Onate had established his colony there, the people were still only nominally Christianised and they had their faith badly shaken when they invoked the power of the Christ child to break a terrible drought.

The growing corn of the Indians began to turn yellow and dry and the water in the river became too low to be led by the irrigation ditches to the new fields which the Indians had made on the higher bank across the river when they gave up their old fields to the Spaniards. Formerly, had such a situation as this arisen, these Indians would have had a great rain-making ceremonial dance and called on their old gods to send them rain. Now, with implicit faith in the magic of the powerful gods of their new friends, the chief of the clans went to the padre at the mission church and asked him to lend them the blessed image of the child Jesus. The padre enquired of them why they wished the image, and the chief of the corn clan answered: 'We wish to carry the child Jesus around the cornfields, so that he can see in what bad condition they now are, and maybe he will have pity on us and send the rain.'

The padre agreed that the Christ child might go, and the Indians carried it with ceremony over all their fields, chanting and pleading with the little image for rain. Then they returned it to the padre at the mission and went home to await results.

Now as sometimes happens in New Mexico in summer, a great cloudburst rose over the Jemez Mountains and swept up the Rio Grande valley. It deluged the Indian fields and beat the corn to the ground, and worse still, hail followed the rain and completed utterly the destruction of the crops.

When the Indians saw what had happened they were very much cast down, for corn was their main staple of diet. That evening the chiefs held a council and early the next morning they again presented themselves before the padre and this time asked that he lend them the image of the Mother Mary. The padre was surprised and enquired the reason for the request. The chiefs hesitated, but on his refusal to lend them the image without explanation, one chief said: 'Padre, we wish to carry the Mother Mary around the fields this morning, so that she can see for herself what a mess her naughty little boy has made of our cornfields.'

The Indians of San Juan say to this day that if you look at the image of Saint Mary in the old mission church there, you can still see on her cheeks traces of the tears she shed from pity when she saw their ruined cornfields.

Ever since that time the San Juan Indians have had respect for the Christian God, but they appeal to their own tribal nature gods when they want rain for their growing corn. Then they dress in the ceremonial costumes as in ancient times and paint themselves with ceremonial colours, and, carrying sprigs of green spruce, they form in long lines and shake gourd rattles filled with seeds, to simulate the rain falling onto the green corn leaves. So they dance from sunrise to sunset to bring down the rain, while nearby a large drum made of a hollowed cottonwood log, covered with rawhide, is beaten to imitate thunder, and a chorus sings the ancient incantations.

Frank G. Applegate
Indian Stories from the Pueblos

John 12:27 has Jesus saying, 'Now comes my hour of heartbreak . . .' as he sees the cross looming. Here is a short excerpt from the writings of John V. Taylor giving a moving story of a modern mother's heartbreak:

A colleague has recently described to me an occasion when a West Indian woman in a London flat was told of her husband's death in a street accident. The shock of grief stunned her like a blow; she sank into the corner of the sofa and sat there rigid and unhearing. For a long time her terrible tranced look continued to embarrass the family, friends and officials who came and went. Then the schoolteacher of one of her children, an Englishwoman, called and, seeing how things were, went and sat beside her. Without a word she threw an arm around the tight shoulders, clasping them with her full strength. The white cheek was thrust hard against the brown. Then as the unrelenting pain seeped through to her, the newcomer's tears began to flow, falling on their two hands linked in the woman's lap. For a long time that is all that was happening. And then at last the West Indian woman started to sob. Still not a word was spoken and after a little while the visitor got up and went, leaving her contribution to help the family meet its immediate needs.

That is the embrace of God, his kiss of life. That is the embrace of his mission, and of our intercession. And the Holy Spirit is the force in the straining muscles of an arm, the film of sweat between pressed cheeks, the mingled wetness on the backs of clasped hands. He is as close and as unobtrusive as that, and as irresistibly strong.

John V. Taylor
The Go-between God

Palm/Passion Sunday

*Mark 11:1-11 or John 12:12-16/
Mark 14:1-15:47 or Mark 15:1-39 (40-47)*

Love in return for costly love is no mean memorial and no small goal for disciples.

'She has done a beautiful (*kalos*) thing to me.' *Kalos* can mean good (morally right) or beautiful (aesthetically pleasing) but in the present context it means more than either of the above. To give to the poor is right (Mark 14:7) but the woman's deed is of a different order of rightness. To anoint the head with perfume is aesthetically pleasing, but the woman's act is of a higher order of beauty. What she does is admirable because it is timely. The beauty of her extravagant and apparently wasteful gesture is due to the particular situation. Jesus is about to die. So we bring flowers to loved ones and friends who are sick, realising suddenly that they will not always be with us.

A further dimension makes the woman's deed admirable: 'she has done what she could,' or literally 'what she had'. This expression, found only in Mark, suggests that what she had, she gave; or what she had it in her power to do, she did. Her act is beautiful because she invested herself in it. She gave what she had to him who was about to give his life for her.

Those who objected to the woman's extravagant act understood well the importance of giving to the poor, but they failed to see something even more important: the beauty and goodness of uncalculating love. They are paradigms of Christians who 'do the right deed for the wrong reason'; examples of those who 'give away all [they] have, and . . . deliver [their] body to be burned, but have not love'; exponents of 'the organised charity, scrimped and iced, in the name of a cautious statistical Christ'. (T. S. Eliot, *Murder in the Cathedral*; 1 Corinthians 13:3; J. B. O'Reilly, *In Bohemia*.)

Christian stewardship as a regular pattern of life is a good and challenging ideal, but this anonymous woman's response to Jesus moves on different grounds. Her deed springs from a personal love for Jesus which, on occasion, breaks all the patterns, defies common sense, and simply gives. Spontaneous, uncalculating, and timely, her gift calls us to love Jesus in this way too and not to judge the way others express their love for him.

That is why 'wherever in all the world the Gospel is proclaimed, what she has done will be told as her memorial'

101

(Mark 14:9 NEB). She left no name, but rather the memory of a beautiful deed. Love in return for costly love is no mean memorial and no small goal for disciples.

Lamar Williamson, Jun.
Mark: Interpretation Bible Commentary

If ever I am disappointed with my lot in life, I stop and think about little Jamie Scott. Jamie was trying for a part in a school play. His mother told me that he'd set his heart on being in it, though she feared he would not be chosen.

On the day the parts were awarded, I went with her to collect him after school. Jamie rushed up, eyes shining with pride and excitement. Then he said those words that remain a lesson to me: 'I've been chose to clap and cheer.'

Marie Curling

Nina was captivated by the story of the nativity, birth and eventual death of Jesus on the cross, and was overjoyed when she was chosen to be an angel in the nativity play. She learnt her lines to perfection. However, Nina is given to adding her own logic to every situation.

The nativity was well under way and when it was her turn to say her lines to Mary, she said: 'Don't worry, Mary, you will have a lovely baby and you will call him Jesus.'

She then added, 'But I wouldn't get too attached to him, 'cos he'll be dead by Easter.'

John Marshall

When tanks roll by and trumpets play
    some people cheer and shout 'Hooray'
    but Jesus chose another way
    parading on a donkey.

He set out to impress them all . . .
    a horse would make him proud and tall
    and save him from the risk of fall . . .
    but he rode on a donkey.

No soldier he, but King of Love!
The way he chose was well above
    all hawkish ways, and as a Dove
    he rode upon a donkey.

Folk must have laughed to see the sight,
    a conqueror who would not fight
    with what is wrong for what is right . . .
    and riding on a donkey.

He had to show that he was brave
    and that he only came to save,
    less like a king, more like a slave,
    for he rode on a donkey.

No matter if the world despise
    this Jesus-way of sacrifice;
    for love lives on when all else dies;
    and he rode on a donkey.

God offered love, not pomp and show,
    so people everywhere would know
    the way his kingdom has to grow;
    so Jesus rode a donkey.

Who cares about the tyrant's pride?
Today Palm Sunday is world-wide
    and millions stand with us, beside
    the king who rode a donkey.

David J. Harding

His master's voice: the shepherd voice

The sheep follow him; for they know his voice (John 10:4). Here is the story of the Good Shepherd told by the Good Shepherd himself.

When I was a boy the most familiar title on a gramophone record was *His Master's Voice*, showing a dog with his ear cocked. Sheep and dogs and animals used by people recognise the voice of the one in charge.

In this verse in particular is described a familiar scene in the life of a Palestinian shepherd. A modern traveller was once involved in a situation where three shepherds brought their flocks to a well. At first they all jostled and got mixed up together. How could anyone separate them out again?

One shepherd started up the valley side and called out, 'Men-ah! Men-ah!' (Arabic for 'Follow me!') His sheep sorted themselves out, gathered together and followed him.

The second shepherd did likewise and called out 'Men-ah! Men-ah!' – the same words as the first shepherd, but a different bunch of sheep sorted themselves out, 'his own'.

The third was about to follow suit but the traveller stopped him, and said, 'Give me your turban and your crook: and see if they will follow me'. The traveller used the same words, 'Men-ah! Follow me!', and tried to imitate the shepherd's voice. In vain, not a sheep moved even its ears! Sheep can look very obviously unimpressed with a peculiarly devastatingly woolly uncomprehending expression!

He tried a second and a third time with the same result. They knew not the voice of the stranger. Then their own shepherd called, devoid of his familiar paraphernalia, without turban or crook, and the sheep scurried after him!

There is the power of the voice. We live with voices more than faces, intensely personal and individual, especially if well-known and dearly loved. I recall once at boarding-school, two or three years after my mother's death, being absolutely alone in the entrance hall at one end of a long corridor and hearing her voice call my name from the other end.

The sheep's knowledge is based on long intimacy, familiar with the shepherd's ways, speech, tones, for years under his command and care, listening to his call.

The pastor, the shepherd, is a peculiar contribution of Christianity. Other religions have priests and preachers, but pastors are a distinctive feature of the Gospel community.

So give them a chance to hear, recognise and respond to the voice of Christ!

Rev. T. D. Meadley (Unpublished sermon)

Easter Day

John 20:1-18 (CWL) or Mark 16:1-8

*We have come
to where the
fragments must
be fused painfully
into a unity by
resurrection out of
a three-days tomb.*

In locations as varied as my bedroom, a girl friend's home, a Texan parsonage, a Spanish night club, the beautiful Lake District and theological college, the risen Christ has appeared personally to me, spoken words of healing, calling and assurance. He has always known my personal inner need, my personal whereabouts, and never failed to minister to my condition. It has been of crucial importance to me to realise that the risen Lord is not confined to Galilee, but is everywhere present and relevant to me.

I feel sure that what is true for me and for millions of Christian people the world over, must also have been true for the beautiful film star named in the following poem. At first sight there appears to be no correlation with a risen Christ, but maybe the ending might make you think again. R. D.

Prayer for Marilyn Monroe

Lord, accept this girl!
Called Marilyn Monroe throughout the world
though that was not her name
(but you know her real name, that of an orphan raped at nine,
the shop girl who tried to kill herself when aged sixteen)
who now goes into your presence without make-up,
without her Press Agent,
without her photographs or signing autographs,
lonely as an astronaut facing the darkness of outer space.

When a girl, she dreamed she was naked in a church
(according to *Time*)
standing in front of a prostrate multitude, heads to the ground,
and had to walk on tiptoe to avoid the heads.
You know our dreams better than all psychiatrists.
Church, house or cave all represent the safety of the womb
but also something more . . .
The heads are admirers, so much is clear, (that mass of heads
in the darkness below the beam to the screen)
but the temple isn't the studios of 20th-Century Fox.
The temple of marble and gold, is the temple of her body

105

in which the Son of Man stands whip in hand
driving out the money-changers of a 20th-Century Fox
who made your house of prayer a den of thieves.

Lord, in this world
contaminated equally by radioactivity and sin,
surely you will not blame a shop girl
who (like any other shop girl) dreamed of being a star?
And her dream became 'reality' (technicolour reality).
All she did was follow the script we gave her,
that of our own lives, but it was meaningless.
Forgive her, Lord, and likewise all of us
for this our twentieth century
and the Mammoth Super-Production in whose making we
    all shared.

She was hungry for love and we offered her tranquillisers.
For the sadness of our not being saints
they recommend psychoanalysis.
Remember, Lord, her increasing terror of the camera
and hatred of make-up (yet insistence on being newly made-up
for every scene) and how the terror grew
and how her unpunctuality at the studios grew.

Like any other shop girl she dreamed of being a star.
And her life was as unreal as a dream an analyst reads and files.
Her romances were kisses with closed eyes
which when the eyes are opened
are seen to have been played out beneath the spotlights
but the spotlights have gone out,
and the two walls of the room (it was a set) are taken down
while the Director moves away, notebook in hand,
the scene being safely canned.
Or like a cruise on a yacht, a kiss in Singapore, a dance in Rio;
a reception in the mansion of the Duke and Duchess of Windsor
viewed in the sad tawdriness of a cheap apartment.
The film ended without a final kiss.
They found her dead in bed, hand on the phone,
and the detectives knew not whom she was about to call.
It was as though someone had dialled the only friendly voice
and heard a pre-recorded tape saying 'WRONG NUMBER'
or like someone wounded by gangsters,
who reaches out towards a disconnected phone.

Lord, whomsoever
it may have been that she was going to call
but did not (and perhaps it was no one at all
or Someone not named in the Los Angeles directory),
Lord, answer that phone.

Ernesto Cardenal
Marilyn Monroe and Other Poems

Death is the physic;
there is no remedy less radical.
We cannot patch the threadbare goodness
with a small square of glory.
We have come to where the fragments must be fused
painfully into a unity
by resurrection out of a three-days tomb.

First, death of self-concern
which stands outside the event
to keep the score of good or bad –
'How am I making out?' – 'That's better now.'
For we must be born into that action which is all ourself,
total commitment when the cost's been weighed;
authentic choice to be, without reserves in case it doesn't work.

The death to judgement of our brother;
the secret pleasure in his faults;
the double-minded condemning while love wrestles to control.

Then last of all, the death to set us free
from testing God, setting the scene where he must play a part.
Dance to our piping,
ratify our schemes because we made him patron;

doing our own will behind the Three-fold Name.
Dead, and alive in Christ
we find new trust.
Not flabby relaxation but poised rest;
the knife edge of discernment's still to tread,
but always with the knowledge that he reigns
both in the choosing and whatever comes
out of that choice.

The grave clothes hold us,
they're all we know.
Give us courage to be loosed and live.

Michael Hare Duke
The Break of Glory

Second Sunday of Easter

John 20:19-31

Galileo was right when he called doubt the father of discovery.

In the vocabulary of religion the word *doubt* has a bad significance. Have you ever heard a preacher use it in a favourable sense? Faith is a great word. Faith is the victory that overcomes the world, and is not doubt its chief enemy? So the word *doubt* has been exiled to religion's semantic doghouse.

But that does not solve the problem. Once more today I feel what I commonly feel when I face worshipping congregations. You look so pious. You are so reverent. You listen so respectfully to Scripture and anthem. You sing so earnestly the resounding hymns. Yet I know and you know that in every life there is something else which our worship does not express – doubts, questions, uncertainties, scepticisms. Every one of us, facing the Christian faith, must honestly say what the man in the Gospel story said to Jesus: 'Lord, I believe; help thou mine unbelief.' . . .

Concerning this problem, which in one way or another we all face, I offer two preliminary observations. First, doubt is not a 'snake', the capacity to doubt is one of man's noblest powers . . . The great servants of our race have been distinguished because in the face of universally accepted falsehoods they dared stand up and cry: 'I doubt that!' Without the capacity to doubt there could be no progress – only docile, unquestioning acceptance of the status quo and its established dogmatisms.

Think of the scientific realm! The earth is flat, the sun circles round it – when such ideas were everywhere accepted, a few bravely dared to disbelieve them. Every scientific advance has started with scepticism. When we think of the scientific pioneers we emphasise their faith, their affirmative belief in new ideas and possibilities. Right! But in the experience of the pioneers themselves their first poignant struggle, their initial critical venture, centred in perilous and daring disbelief. Galileo was right when he called doubt the father of discovery.

. . . Jesus himself was a magnificent doubter. Wild ideas of a war-making Messiah who would overthrow Rome were prevalent in his time. He doubted them. 'An eye for an eye and a tooth for a tooth' was the true law, they said. He doubted it. He saw men trusting in long prayers, broad phylacteries, rigid Sabbath rules, dietary laws as essential to true religion, and he doubted them all. He saw men believing in ancient traditions just because they were ancient, and he poured his scepticism on such reactionaries: 'It was said unto them of old time, but I say unto you . . .' Samaritans are an inferior race was the popular idea, but he scorned it; a good Samaritan, he said, is better than a bad priest. We are saved by Jesus' faith, we say. Yes, but just as truly as any scientific pioneer did, he reached his faith through his daring doubts. My friends, we sing the praises of the great believers. So do I. But who can worthily express our unpayable indebtedness to the brave doubters, who in perilous times, when false ideas dominated men's minds and spoiled their lives, saved the day with their courageous disbelief? Let us sing their praises too!

My second preliminary observation is that the sturdiest faith has always come out of the struggle with doubt. There are only two ways in which we can possess the Christian faith. One is to inherit it, borrow it, swallow it without question, take it over as we do the cut of our clothes without thinking about it. Some here may be able to do that, but your faith then is not really *yours*. You never fought for it. As one student said: 'Being a Methodist, just because your parents were, is like wearing a secondhand hat that does not fit.' No! Great faith, if it is really to be one's very own, always has to be fought for.

One who does not understand this, does not understand the Bible. It is a book of faith, we say. To be sure it is! But it is also a book filled with the struggles of men wrestling with their doubts and unbelief. Listen to Gideon crying, 'If the Lord is with us, why then has all this befallen us?' Listen to the Psalmist: 'My tears have been my food day and night, while they continually say unto me, where is thy God?'

. . . Indeed, listen to our Lord himself on Calvary! He is quoting the twenty-second psalm. He knows it by heart. 'My God, my God, why hast thou forsaken me? Why art thou so far from helping me?' I am talking to someone here who is struggling with his doubts. The Bible is your book, my friend. All its faith was hammered out on the hard anvil of doubt.

. . . Today I emphasise one central matter in the experience of the great believers: they went honestly through with their disbeliefs until at last they began to doubt their doubts. How important that process is! When it was first suggested that steamships could be built which could cross the ocean, multitudes were sceptical. One man proved it could not be done. He wrote a book proving that no steamship could carry enough fuel to keep its engines going across the ocean. Well, the first steamship that crossed the Atlantic and landed in

New York harbour carried a copy of that book. Ah, my sceptical disbeliever, you would have been a wiser man had you carried your doubt a little further until you doubted your doubts! I am preaching this sermon because I want someone here not to stop doubting but to go through with his scepticism until he disbelieves his disbelief.

... Robert Louis Stevenson became a man of radiant faith, but he did not start that way. He started by calling the religion he was brought up in 'the deadliest gag and wet blanket that can be laid on man'. He started by calling himself 'a youthful atheist'. Then, as he grew up, began what Gilbert Chesterton called his 'first wild doubts of doubt'. 'The church was not right,' wrote Stevenson, 'but certainly not the antichurch either.' 'Tis a strange world,' he said, 'but there is a manifest God for those who care to look for him.' Then at last he began talking about his 'cast-iron faith'. 'Whether on the first day of January or the thirty-first of December,' he wrote, 'faith is a good word to end on.' So he went through with his scepticism until he found his disbelief unbelievable.

Harry Emerson Fosdick
The Importance of Doubting our Doubts

Third Sunday of Easter

Luke 24:36b-48

*The person of
the risen Christ
does not dissolve,
but remains
unmistakably a
concrete figure,
a definite person.*

Hardly any artist can match the power of artistic and religious expression of one who, though influenced both by the Italian Renaissance and Dutch painting, now depicted in a highly independent new way not only the crucified Christ but also the risen Christ: Matthias Grunewald. . . . On the reverse of his Isenheim altar, on the other side of his crucified Christ, he also painted the risen Christ.

One can only guess what this picture-book leaf, opened on festivals, must have meant for the lepers of Isenheim – covered in sores and blisters – as an image of the hope of a clean, whole body. What inner radiance there is in the colours which shine from it! The resurrection is depicted as a cosmic event, not against a golden background but against the black night sky with a few shining stars. In a powerful surge the risen Christ is soaring with arms uplifted, taking the white gravecloth with him, surrounded by an enormous radiance of light which turns into the colours of the rainbow and changes the cloth first into blue, then into violet, and in the centre into flaming red and yellow. What a symphony of colours! And that is the unique thing about this Easter picture: an unusual degree of spiritualisation is achieved, and yet the body of the transfigured Christ remains clearly visible: the person of the risen Christ does not dissolve, but remains unmistakably a concrete figure, a definite person. The wound-marks on the alabastine body and the scarlet mouth recall that this is none other that the crucified Christ who – with the gesture of blessing and revelation – is entering the sphere of pure light. The face of the risen Christ, right in the centre, sunny, with an inner radiance, goes over into the blinding yellow of the aureole, which is like a sun. And though the outlines of the face are blurred by the shining light, with great tranquillity a pair of eyes look towards the beholder with gentle authority and reconciling grace. Truly, if an artist has ever succeeded in indicating in colour something that cannot really be painted, namely the *soma pneumatikon*, as the apostle Paul calls it, the 'pneumatic body', the spiritual body of the risen Christ, it is Grunewald.

Hans Kung
Credo

In Luke's telling of the resurrection narratives, several themes are recurrent and vital to the whole message of the early Christian writer. . . . A theme considered [earlier] was the importance of eating together for Jesus' work and the mission of the church. However, in Luke 24:39-43, another dimension of eating is added. Here Jesus' act of eating fish, joined with his offering of his hands and feet for examination, says something about the resurrection. By insisting on the corporeality of the risen Christ, Luke is saying no to those forms of Christology that said Jesus only 'seemed' (Docetism) to be human. Even the resurrected Jesus says, 'Touch me and see; for a ghost does not have flesh and bones as you see I have' (verse 39). Luke is also saying no to those doctrines of resurrection that were really pagan notions of the immortality of the spirit. Christians believe in the resurrection of the dead, not escape into a spirit world. And Luke is saying no to those notions of spirituality that view the body and all things physical as inherently inferior or evil. Those who view themselves as just passing through this evil world tend to neglect the physical, economic and political needs of other human beings. Luke reminds us that the risen Christ said, 'Look at my wounds,' and 'Do you have anything to eat?' No one can follow this Christ and say that discipleship means being only concerned with 'souls'.

. . . In comments on Easter Day we reflected upon the restraint of New Testament writers in the use of this material. Let us add a second word to that description – realism. This may not seem accurate at first, given the appearance of dazzling angels and of Jesus suddenly present and just as suddenly gone. But focus upon the believers to whom Jesus appeared: how realistically they are portrayed! They took resurrection stories as idle tales; they were startled, frightened and confused; they 'disbelieved for joy'. Minds and hearts raced. What does this mean? Do we continue where we left off? Do we begin anew? Will Jesus now go to God and leave us here alone? What will happen to us? Will anybody believe this? Will we be resurrected as Jesus was? These are realistic Easter thoughts, and the preacher who lives among these questions and treats them with respect is more the pastor than the one who misses the pathos and solemnity of resurrection joy.

Fred B. Craddock
Preaching Through the Christian Year: 'B'

Fourth Sunday of Easter

John 10:11-18

*Embrace life
and really live.*

This version of Psalm 23 is a Japanese one.

The Lord is my pace setter; I shall not rush.
He makes me stop and rest for quiet intervals.
He provides me with images of stillness,
    which restore my serenity.
He leads me in ways of efficiency through
    calmness of mind, and his guidance is peace.
Even though I have a great many things to accomplish each day,
    I will not fret, for his presence is here.
His timelessness, his all-importance, will keep me in balance.
He provides refreshment and renewal in the midst of
    my activity
by anointing my mind with his oils of tranquillity.
My cup of joyous energy overflows.
Surely harmony and effectiveness shall be the fruits
    of my hours,
for I shall walk in the pace of my Lord and dwell in his
    house for ever.

Sometimes life seems to be one mad rush. I find myself at times having to fit so many things into a day. So I dash from place to place, calling at the prison and the hospital, the bakery, where I'm part-time chaplain, conducting business meetings and keeping in touch with the uniformed organisations of the church. At the end of the day I usually heave a great sigh of relief and look forward to a good night's sleep. The trouble is I know that tomorrow will be the same again, business and rush as usual. So I sometimes ask myself, 'how do I keep my balance?' And whenever I ask this I think back over thirty years to the time when I worked as a stagehand at a variety theatre. Among the many different acts I saw, only one stands out. It was a husband and wife team from South America. The husband used to balance on a tightrope. He was blindfold and used to throw long knives at a revolving target upon which his wife was strapped by her wrists and ankles. I saw the act twice nightly for six nights and was always amazed that the knives missed the lady, but even more amazed by the way in which the man kept his balance. One night I tried to balance on the tightrope but soon fell off.

Keeping your balance in the business of living is also difficult at times. In this Japanese version of Psalm 23 there are hints given about the secret of doing so. Let God set the pace. Stop and rest with him for quiet intervals. Think of him, meditate on his goodness and mercy. In doing so something of his serenity, his balance, will come to you. May this be so for you today.

Ron Dale
Pause for Thought

I have included the part of the theological analysis of *Dead Poets Society* which follows because for me the film opened my eyes to a wider understanding of what being a 'good shepherd' meant in terms of educating young people.

Robin Williams played the part of Keating, a charismatic English teacher who sought to widen his students' horizons, release them from the restricting confines of family and school expectations and encourage each student to 'seize the day' when new opportunities arose in their lives. He encouraged them to take responsibility and become their true selves: to embrace life and really live.

It all reminded me of the words of Jesus: 'I am the Good Shepherd' and 'I am come that they might have life, and have it abundantly.'

Ron Dale

Background to the film

Dead Poets Society draws on several different film genres for its inspiration. Its academic milieu places it alongside such films as *Blackboard Jungle* (Richard Brooks, 1955), *To Sir, With Love* (James Clavell, 1966), *Dangerous Minds* (John N. Smith,

1995), and *Mr Holland's Opus* (Stephen Herek, 1995). In placing a teacher at the centre of its narrative, *Dead Poets Society* also echoes *Goodbye Mr Chips* (Sam Wood, 1939), *The Browning Version* (Anthony Asquith, 1951), and *The Prime of Miss Jean Brodie* (Ronald Neame, 1969). As a study of teenage angst, Weir's film follows, albeit at a safe distance, *The Wild One* (Laslo Benedek, 1953), *Rebel Without a Cause* (Nicholas Ray, 1955), *Running Scared* (David Hemmings, 1972), and a whole series of 1950s 'juvenile delinquent' movies such as *The Delinquents* (Robert Altman, 1957), *Dangerous Youth* (Herbert Wilcox, 1958), and *Young and Wild* (William Witney, 1958).

Peter Weir was one of the main protagonists behind the Australian film industry's renaissance in the late 1970s. After studying law he moved into television production and subsequently into film. Prior to making *Dead Poets Society*, Weir had directed eight feature films. These earlier works offer clues as to the 'preferred' meaning(s) which may be encoded within the text of *Dead Poets Society*. The struggle of the individual against society and its institutions is a major theme linking many of Weir's narratives. In *Picnic at Hanging Rock* (1975) the repressive educational system of Appleyard College causes the same kind of problems for a group of turn-of-the-century Australian schoolgirls that Welton Academy poses for Neil and his friends in the late 1950s; *Gallipoli* (1981) investigates a different form of institutional confinement – life in the military services, and *Witness* (1985) probes the often suffocating conformity inherent within an Amish community. Thus the individualist philosophy which permeates the narrative of *Dead Poets Society* has precedents in Weir's earlier work. The origin of this philosophy may lie in the Australian's personal resistance to conformity: 'I can't try to fit in with some sort of system', and in his interest in Jungian psychology with its references to dreams and visions, all of which are in evidence within the narrative of *Dead Poets Society*.

Although, as Giroux correctly argues, Weir has invested *Dead Poets Society* with 'an aura of universality', many of the moral and ethical issues which the film confronts can be seen to grow out of and reflect specificities inherent in late 1950s American society. Keating's individualism can be seen as a reaction against a decade marked by cultural philistinism and the persecution of intellectual non-conformists. In its attempt to counterpoint the restrictive political and ideological philosophies of Eisenhower and McCarthy, *Dead Poets Society* arguably portrays a sense of the first flickerings of a new sensibility, a sensibility which would only fully ignite in the 1960s.

A preferred reading

The film's narrative works extremely hard in its attempt to persuade the viewer to accept Keating as a sincere, charismatic purveyor of existentialist philosophy. Why would one be tempted to question any of the motives of Mr. Keating? The English teacher's extraordinary entrance follows an opening sequence which includes a montage of vignettes which reflect the cornerstones of Welton's educational philosophy – 'tradition', 'honour', 'discipline' and 'excellence'. Alongside this montage, Weir presents a powerful visual metaphor, which in essence signifies the film's central theme – the freedom, or lack of freedom of the individual. For example, as the boys prepare for the first day of the new semester, the director offers a series of wide-angle shots of hundreds of birds in flight against a background of rolling countryside and expansive sky. These spacious scenes are juxtaposed with a tightly packed shot of boys moving up and down a spiral staircase. As the boys hurry to their lessons, the camera rotates through 360 degrees to produce a shot which allows the viewer to experience their sense of claustrophobia. The atmosphere in the classrooms is equally stifling as Hager, the trigonometry teacher, sets his charges copious amounts of homework, and McAllister, the classics teacher, is seen regimenting rote learning of Latin verbs. Into this cauldron of conformity steps John Keating who immediately disorientates his students by taking them outside the confines of the classroom for what is essentially an initiation into the world of the 'free thinker'. From this point on Keating becomes the boys' spiritual leader, their 'Captain', coaxing and inspiring them to take the path to self-fulfilment and to rail against the harmful, homogenising effects of society's institutions.

Robin Williams is instrumental in extending and developing Keating's charismatic persona. No stranger to playing unconventional characters, Williams had previously portrayed the eccentric T. S. Garp in *The World according to Garp* (George Roy Hill, 1982), and the establishment-threatening Adrian Cronauer in *Good Morning, Vietnam* (Barry Levinson, 1987). As in these earlier films, Williams utilises his considerable improvisational skills in his portrayal of John Keating, often interpreting the script in his own idiosyncratic way. Like the boys, the viewer may be captivated by Keating's rhetoric as he persuades us to 'suck the marrow out of life', and to make our lives 'extraordinary'; we too may emotionally bond with the teacher as he invites us to 'huddle up' in order to share his wisdom; and we may share the joy experienced by Keating and his students as their triumph on the soccer field is glorified by the spirit-lifting final movement of Beethoven's *Choral Symphony*.

As Giroux has argued, prior to the arrival of Keating, *Dead Poets Society* appears to present the boys as 'academic zombies living out the projections and wishes of their . . . fathers'. At Welton 'The Law of the Father' dominates in what is essentially a patriarchal environment. Paradoxically however, none of the featured students benefits from having an understanding father in whom they can confide their innermost thoughts. Neil's father is dogmatically unbending in his attempt to control his son's life, while in contrast, Todd's father appears to be totally uninterested, the duplicated birthday present functioning as a symbolic representation of the lack of intimacy between them. Ripping pages out of textbooks and reciting poetry in caves may not appear to be excessively revolutionary behaviour, yet, in the context of intensive parental and institutional pressure to conform, the boys' actions, as they strive towards realising their own self-identities, can be seen as something more than mere tokenism.

Clearly, therefore, the 'preferred' reading of the film suggests that Keating is a type of 'saviour' figure to those he teaches. We see a person of uncompromising commitment and enthusiasm, able to inspire in the young a view of life which sees in every moment of every day, the opportunity to live life to the full. *Carpe diem* is breathed into the very core and fibre of the students in his care. Such exhortations are not simply an appeal to the intellect, but to the whole person: heart, body, mind and spirit. Here education is concerned with developing individual potential, with the emphasis placed on encouraging personal conviction and individual choice. All the scenes which show ritual conformity (whether in the classroom, revealing an instrumental approach towards the teaching of poetry, or comically in the school grounds, where the students are encouraged not to walk in step, but to march in their own way), persuade the viewer that student-centred learning is being put into practice. For too long Welton has produced an unfair and elitist system. Now things are about to change and the time has arrived for a truly liberal education, based on the finest ideals and values, to undercut a system which arguably perpetuates a crippling orthodoxy based on conformity and rigid discipline. Keating is to be emulated as a model teacher rather than questioned or criticised for his unorthodox teaching methods or motives.

Conclusion

Dead Poets Society can be seen as both an endorsement of individualism and the romantic spirit, and as a critique of the dangers inherent in such a philosophy. The film raises serious and problematic ethical questions for Christians in respect of how to understand suicide. Is Neil's suicide an act of heroism which draws attention to the injustices of the world and through which others might learn, or is it simply a misguided act of folly, selfish to the extreme? Similarly, it is never easy for the viewer to discern whether Keating was exercising extraordinary Christian courage in his adoption of the radical methods he employed with his pupils, or whether, in truth, he was largely motivated by a wrongheaded and proud determination to shock. The 'right action' to take in such schools as Welton Academy is never given a clear-cut answer in *Dead Poets Society*. For example, it might be argued that Mr Keating always tried to behave according to the principles of Christian love, or *agape*, and that this is shown most vividly in his insistence that pupils must be given opportunities and advice to achieve their full potential. Christian *agape* always demands that one tries to work for the good of the other person without reserve or distinction, unconditionally. Barclay writes that *agape* is 'an undefeatable attitude of goodwill . . . an attitude of goodwill to others no matter what they are like'. In a similar way, the exhortation to 'seize the day' could be said to reflect a distinctively biblical emphasis about living life to the full, rooted in an embrace, not a denial, of the God-given goodness of creation. In Mr Keating's concern that his pupils relish the sweetness of every moment, some Christian viewers might recognise a strongly New Testament emphasis. For example, the Johannine theme, 'I came that they may have life, and have it abundantly' (John 10:10) and the Matthean emphasis in the Sermon on the Mount about not worrying about tomorrow (Matthew 6:34) point to obvious overlaps with Mr Keating's approach to and philosophy of life. Similarly, in his pupils' responsive endeavours to free themselves from any oppressive external constraints, they may be said to reflect a biblical understanding of human personhood since, having been made in the image of their Creator, they become determined to pursue lives of dignity, truthfulness and freedom (Genesis 1:27).

However, although the radical demands of love underpin Christian notions of moral motivation and action, no easy or uncontested answers to the most appropriate ways of behaving in specific situations have ever been given by

Christians. Those trying to act out of Christian love still require gifts of discernment and insight in order that their actions may reflect those of Christ in the new and challenging circumstances in which they and others find themselves. Therefore, love which is superficially formed and simply content to 'mean well' is often claimed to be irresponsible, unhelpful and potentially dangerous. For example, Preston suggests that this ability to reflect on the possible consequences of certain types of action is one of the most important elements in developing an approach to Christian living. He comments: 'Some of the worst sins against love have been perpetrated by those who "meant well".' This point is well taken in relation to our consideration of the 'Christian' nature of Mr Keating's action. Even if we sense that throughout the film his motivation is pure, there is always a feeling too that his well-meaning exhortations are somewhat immature and his judgements not always wise. Mr Keating might well have believed that what he was advocating to his pupils had the potential to change their lives for ever and for the good, but his lack of discernment and incapacity to foresee the possible consequences of his 'philosophy' might betray a significant lack of spiritual depth or awareness for some Christian viewers.

As we have said, the film gives neither any clear-cut answers, nor, therefore, a simple 'Christian' message. The film's inherent ambivalence and tension should not, however, disappoint us. For its strength and success surely reside in its portrayal of ethical ambiguity and contradiction.

Edited by Clive Marsh and Gaye Ortiz
Explorations in Theology and Film
(The quote was written by Stephen Brie and David Torvell and entitled *Moral Ambiguity and Contradiction in* Dead Poets Society.)

Fifth Sunday of Easter

John 15:1-8

The fruit which the disciples are expected to bear is not merely excellencies of character, but a will and capacity for service.

We are the members of Christ, and Christ is our member. And my hand, the hand of one who is the poorest of the poor, is Christ, and my foot is Christ. And I, the poorest of the poor, am the hand of Christ and the foot of Christ. I move my hand and Christ moves, who is my hand. For you must know that divinity is undivided. I move my foot and my foot shines as he shines. Do not say that this is blasphemy, but confirm this, and adore Christ who has made you in this way. For you also, if such is your desire, will become one of his members. And so all the members of each one of us will become the members of Christ, and Christ our member, and he will make all that is ugly and ill-shapen, beautiful and well-shapen, in that he adorns it with the splendour and majesty of his Godhead. And we shall all become gods and intimately united with God, and our bodies will seem to us immaculate, and since we have partaken of the semblance of the whole body of Christ, each one of us shall possess all of Christ. For the one who has become many remains the one undivided, but each part is all of Christ.

Symeon the Younger
Anthony P. Castle: *More Quotes and Anecdotes*

The Vine and the Branches, John 15:1-6.

Verses 1, 2. In the language of the prophets, the nation is spoken of as God's 'vine' or 'vineyard' (Isaiah 5:1-7; Jeremiah 2:21; Ezekiel 15:1-6; 19:10-14; Psalm 80:8-16). Compare also Matthew 7:16-20; 12:33; 20:1; 21:28-43. *The true vine* and its *branches* represent together the new society, in which all the care and promises of God given to the ancient chosen nation come to fulfilment. The speaker has in mind not only the individual's relation to himself, but his membership of the new society, the

Church. *The true vine* is the vine that *bears fruit* (verses 4, 5). Israel has not borne fruit (cf. Matthew 21:19). *He cleanseth it* (R.V.), rather 'pruneth it'. The denial of Peter and the experience it brought him was his 'pruning' that he might *bear more fruit*. The *fruit* which the disciples are expected to bear is not merely excellencies of character, but a will and capacity for service.

They are sent out on a mission to bring others into the community. Theirs is the mission on which the Father had sent his Son (15:16; 17:18; 4:38). Judas forfeited his mission and became a *withered* branch (verse 6). He is 'cast out' in the same act as *when he went out and it was night* (13:30; 3, 4 cf. 6:37). The other disciples are *clean*. Jesus has given them his *word*, which is the Word made flesh, i.e. the personal word of God (17:14). They abide in him. These men are ennobled and cleansed by their mission and message. Verse 3 and 13:10 should be pondered together. 'Jesus washed the feet of those that were clean, and to those to whom he promised cleansing, he said, "Ye are clean"' (Schlatter). Underlying the thought, there is the conception of Jesus as judge. He alone can pronounce men *clean*. His is a divine prerogative. Unfruitfulness alone separates men from Christ and his Church. The Church without a sense of mission is no church. A similar idea underlies Paul's conception of Christians as 'the body of Christ'. Through our bodies we make contact with the outer world.

The Mission of the New Society, John 15:7-16

Verse 7. *If . . . my words abide in you*. Note the substitution of *my words* for 'I' of verse 5. It was through his *words* that these men experienced the power of his personality. His *words* are the Word of God, and do not cut the air and vanish. They 'accomplish the thing whereto they are sent' (Isaiah 55:11; cf. 14:10; 6:63). Note the recurrence of the same conjunction of ideas in verses 7 and 8 as in 14:12-14.

R. H. Strachan
The Fourth Gospel: The Farewell Discourses. Part II, xv-xvi.

Sixth Sunday of Easter

John 15:9-17

Friendship is nothing else than a complete union of feeling on all subjects, divine and human, accompanied by kindly feeling and attachment.

Coming in silence

'We were friends who understood each other totally,' Rostropovich says of Shostakovich the 'deep and introverted' composer. The nature of that friendship can be heard not just in the words spoken by Rostropovich's interpreter during our interview, but in the cellist's tone of voice in Russian and in his excursions into eccentrically broken but unusually expressive English.

He gives an example of their friendship. In the 1950s there were times when, late at night, there would be telephone calls from Shostakovich. 'Slava, Slava,' the composer would plead, using Rostropovich's familiar name, 'immediately, you have to come see me. Immediately, I need you to come.'

'I think to myself,' says Rostropovich, 'maybe he wants to speak about some concert coming up – because at that time we went on some small tours together. He would play the piano, and I the cello in performance of his music. So I would go to him. And he would move a chair over to his desk, just the way we are sitting now, and say, "Sit, Slava, sit".' Rostropovich leans forward, imitating the composer's welcoming gesture, combining need and conspiratorial friendship. 'And then he would say, "Slava, now let's just be quiet".' Slava sits before me for a moment, the pause lending emphasis to the point. 'And we'd sit there not looking at each other. It was like an eternity. First of all, I was still young. Can you imagine? I go without a single word for the span of fifteen minutes? And then he would get up and say, "Thank you, thank you, Slava, for coming to see me". And I would go.'

Why the silence? 'He just needed human warmth. Somebody who would radiate warmth, who would understand everything that was happening to him without explanation. So he wouldn't need words, wouldn't need to say anything. That's the way I explain it. And I would leave and also have a feeling of relief. Somehow we relieved each other.'

Edward Rothstein
From *The Independent Sunday Magazine*

I can only urge you to prefer friendship to all human possessions; for there is nothing so suited to our nature, so well adapted to prosperity or adversity. Friendship is superior to relationship, because from relationship benevolence can be withdrawn, and from friendship it cannot: for with the withdrawal of benevolence the very name of friendship is done away, while that of relationship remains. Friendship is nothing else than a complete union of feeling on all subjects, divine and human, accompanied by kindly feeling and attachment; than which, indeed, I am not aware whether, with the exception of wisdom, anything better has been bestowed on man. Some men prefer riches, others good health, others influence, others again honours, many prefer even pleasures. What, however, can be more delightful than to have one to whom you can speak on all subjects just as to yourself: where would be the great enjoyment in prosperity, if you had not one to rejoice in it equally with yourself: and adversity would indeed be difficult to endure without someone who would bear it even with greater regret than yourself. In short, all other objects that are sought after are severally suited to one single purpose: riches, that you may spend them; power, that you may be courted; honours, that you may be extolled; pleasures, that you may enjoy them; good health, that you may be exempt from harm and perform all the functions of the body. Whereas friendship comprises the greatest number of objects possible; wherever you turn yourself, it is at hand; shut out of no place, never out of season, never irksome; and therefore we do not use fire and water, as they say, on more occasions that we do friendship.

Cicero
De Amicitia

And joy is everywhere; it is in the earth's green covering of grass; in the blue serenity of the sky; in the reckless exuberance of the spring; in the severe abstinence of grey winter; in the living flesh that animates our bodily frame; in the perfect poise of the human figure noble and upright; in living; in the exercise of all our powers; in the acquisition of knowledge; in fighting evils; in dying for gains we never can share. Joy is there everywhere; it is superfluous, unnecessary; nay, it very often contradicts the most peremptory behests of necessity. It exists to show that the bonds of law can only be explained by love; they are like body and soul. Joy is the realisation of the truth of oneness, the oneness of our soul with the world and of the world's soul with the supreme lover.

Sir Rabindranath Tagore
Sadhana

Seventh Sunday of Easter

John 17:6-19

'They have been with Jesus'. The mark and seal of his character is upon them.

At the onset of World War Two, Ernest Gordon joined the Argyll and Sutherland Highlanders. At the age of twenty-four he was captured by the Japanese while escaping from Sumatra after the fall of Singapore. With other British prisoners he was marched into the jungle to build the notorious bridge on the river Kwai.

After terrible suffering and hardship he records: 'We had no church, no chaplain, no services. If there were men who kept faith alive in their hearts they gave no visible sign. At Changi many had turned to religion for the first time. But the crutch had not supported them; so they had thrown it away. Many had prayed, but only for themselves. Nothing happened. They sought personal miracles – and none had come. They had appealed to God as an expedient. But God had apparently refused to be treated as one.

'We had long since resigned ourselves to being derelicts. We were forsaken men – forsaken by our friends, our families, by our Government. Now even God seemed to have left us! . . .'

Some time later Ernest Gordon was approached by a fellow prisoner, an Australian sergeant who asked if he would lead some sort of discussion about the Christian faith, wondering if there was something in Christianity that they had failed to understand.

Very reluctantly Ernest Gordon agreed, even though he had many a doubt and many past experiences that had put him off the faith.

Previously he said: 'I had reached the conclusion that Jesus Christ was a figure in a kind of fairy story, suitable for children perhaps, but not for men.

'The logical place for me to begin now, I reflected, was with the New Testament, as the only record we have of his life and teaching. I had a Bible, an old one that had been given to me by a kindly other rank, who wished to lighten his pack as he set out for a trip farther up-country. It was well thumbed, torn and patched with covers made from the oilskin of a gas cape. There were no references, explanations or annotations.

'That Bible was all I had to draw on when I faced the group next evening in the bamboo grove. I was not a little dismayed to see that there were several dozen of them. They were waiting for me in respectful silence. But their faces said plainly, "We'll tolerate you, chum, so long as you don't try any waffling." (*Waffling* being the gentle art of evading the issue, or making a half-lie take the place of the whole truth.)

'I began by describing my own uncertain state of grace, telling them frankly of my doubts and conflicts. When I asked them straight out if they were willing to go along with me, they said that they were . . .

'Through our readings and discussion we gradually came to know Jesus. He was one of us. He would understand our problems, because they were the kind of problems he had faced himself. Like us, he often had no place to lay his head, no food for his belly, no friends in high places. He, too, had known bone weariness from too much toil; the suffering, the rejection, the disappointments that make up the fabric of life. Yet he was no killjoy. He would not have scorned the man who took a glass of wine with his friends, or a mug of McEwan's ale, or who smiled approvingly at a pretty girl. The friends he had were like our own and like us.

'As we read and talked, he became flesh and blood. Here was a working man, yet one who was perfectly free, who had not been enslaved by society, economics, law or religion. Demonic forces had existed then as now. They had sought to destroy him but they had not succeeded.

'True, he had been suspended on a cross and tormented with the hell of pain; but he had not been broken. The weight of law and of prejudice had borne down on him, but failed to crush him. He had remained free and alive, as the resurrection affirmed. What he was, what he did, all made sense to us. We understood that the love expressed so supremely in Jesus was God's love – the same love that we were experiencing for ourselves – the love that is passionate kindness, other-centred rather than self-centred, greater than all the laws of men . . .

'The doctrines we worked out were meaningful to us. We approached God through Jesus, the carpenter of Nazareth, the incarnate Word. Such an approach seemed logical, for that was the way he had come to us. He had taken flesh, walked in the midst of men and declared himself by his actions to be full of grace and truth.

'We arrived at our understanding of God's ways not one by one, but together. In the fellowship of freedom and love we found truth, and with truth a wonderful sense of unity, of harmony, of peace.'

Ernest Gordon
Miracle on the River Kwai

127

There are some men and women in whose company we are always at our best. While with them we cannot think mean thoughts or speak ungenerous words. Their mere presence is elevation, purification, sanctity. . . . Suppose that influence prolonged through a month, a year, a lifetime and what could not life become? To live with Socrates must have made one wise; with Aristides, just; with Francis of Assisi, gentle. But to have lived with Christ? To have lived with Christ must have made one like Christ; that is to say a Christian.

As a matter of fact, to live with Christ did produce this effect . . . a few raw, uninspiring men were admitted to the inner circle of his friendship. The change began at once. Day by day we can almost see the first disciples grow. First there steals over them the faintest possible adumbration of his character, and occasionally, very occasionally, they do a thing, or say a thing that they could not have done or said had they not been living there. Slowly the spell of his life deepens. Reach after reach of their nature is overtaken, thawed, subjugated, sanctified. Their manners soften, their words become more gentle, their conduct more unselfish. As swallows who have found a summer, as frozen buds the spring, their starved humanity bursts into fuller life. They do not know how it is, but they are different men. One day they find themselves like their Master, going about doing good. To themselves it is unaccountable, but they cannot do otherwise. They were not told to do it, it came to them to do it. But the people who watch them know well how to account for it – 'They have been with Jesus'. The mark and seal of his character is upon them.

Henry Drummond
The Changed Life

Pentecost

John 15:26-27; 16:4b-15

The strange spirit which is God at work freeing people from what restricts and oppresses them will not be bound by human institutions.

Shirley Valentine is a 'woman of spirit'. Though wavering and initially uncertain as to whether to join her friend Jane on a trip to Greece, she has the guts to go. Jane leaves Shirley to fend for herself for the first part of the holiday, but Shirley finds her feet, comforted by her speaking to the rock on the beach – an echo of her talking to the kitchen wall at home. She confronts herself, 'finds herself' again, being able to reassess, in middle age, where the last twenty years have gone. She reviews her life, the loss of her youthful vigour, and the relative loss of a carefree approach to life which she and Joe, her husband, had enjoyed. She ponders what Joe has become. In allowing herself to be seduced by Costas, she retains control of herself to the extent that she finds her freedom again – this is what she wants. She also loses control in the sense that she rediscovers the positive dimension of 'letting go' of herself.

Shirley Valentine can be read in a number of ways. It is a study of middle age, especially of the reappraisals of married life which many middle-aged married people are compelled by changing circumstances to conduct. It is an exploration of a woman's experience to self-discovery. . . . It is a gentle comedy. . . . Though it struggles through a tension between form and content to declare how seriously it wishes to be taken, the film nevertheless raises some key issues about human living. In particular, it addresses questions, and offers tentative answers, about the spiritual resources which human beings require, and reveal themselves as possessing or receiving, in order to be able to handle seemingly ordinary, but demanding issues of human interrelationship.

The basic contours for a discussion of the role of the Spirit of God in human life which this film offers will first be sketched, before being explored in more depth in due course. Three aspects can be highlighted. First, the fact of Shirley praying should not go unnoticed. When about to leave for Greece, in the midst of her own reservations about the consequences of her actions – shared before God – she utters a genuine intercessory prayer. 'God. God, I know . . . I'm bein' cruel, an' I know I'll have to pay for it, when I get back. And I don't mind paying for it then. But just . . . just do me a favour, God, an' don't make me pay for it durin' the two weeks. Keep everyone safe. Please.'

Second, Shirley's quest for freedom can be examined from the perspective of the experience of God as Spirit. Much is made in the film of Shirley's loss of freedom since the days when she was Shirley Bradshaw. Either marriage itself has inevitably proved restrictive, or Shirley has allowed marriage to stifle her. The title song of the film *(The Girl Who Used To Be Me)*, announces from the outset the theme of flying as freedom; flying away to Greece, yet also rising above her present situation in order to examine it. The film begins to consider the implications of her actions (going to Greece, becoming involved with Costas) and thus prevents her flight becoming a form of sheer escapism. It does not go far in this direction. But in delivering an ambiguous ending – it is not clear that all things will be well and that Shirley and Joe will even be re-united (i.e. the quest for freedom is not simple) – the film's treatment of the subject provides resource material for a careful examination of the nature of human freedom. Above all, the film poses the question of the origin and nature of the resources (e.g. the power of personal reflection and self-analysis, inner strength) upon which this quest for freedom is based.

Third, the quest for relationship which unites the first two theological aspects highlighted – Shirley's prayer and her quest for freedom – should also be considered. It is not wholly clear that Shirley wants Joe any more. She is unlikely to leave him. She will make do. But she longs for him to be more the fun-loving Joe she knew when they first met. Her reflection of their early relationship borders on the nostalgic, yet expresses a present need in her too: she has lost the fun-loving side to her. Her relationship with Jane is more of a release, a safe place where she can be more herself. That relationship mirrors earlier 'nights out with the girls'. But Jane's fickleness only emphasises Shirley's aloneness. Shirley's contact with her daughter (Millandra) and her daughter's friend (Sharon-Louise), though representing on Shirley's part a further attempt to recreate a lost past, only emphasises the cultural and age gap between them. Shirley lacks satisfying relationships in a number of directions. However self-seeking his own motivation may have been, Costas fills the gap and enables Shirley to have an immediate (sexual) need met, in a way which spurs on her general reassessment of who she is both as an individual and in relation to others.

These three features in the film provide, then, a basis for a dialogue with Christian theology about a contemporary understanding of spirit. The fact that Christian theology would unavoidably address issues of prayer, freedom and relationship in its discussion of the presence and action of the Spirit of God in contemporary human life makes the film a useful discussion partner . . .

We must reflect further upon the Spirit as the Spirit of freedom. Again, it is no coincidence that the Christian tradition has explored the notion of freedom. . . . The Spirit in Christian theology has symbolised release and free expression in individual experience and in corporate worship, building upon insights which reverberate through the Bible (e.g. 1 Samuel 19:19-24; John 8:31-36; 14:25-27; 15:26; 1 Corinthians 12; 2 Corinthians 3:17). This has frequently led to the opposite of what the Apostle Paul was struggling to emphasise to the Corinthian Church. Instead of the unity that was needed as the expression of oneness in Christ, the strangeness of the Spirit's effects upon believers often seemed to cause disunity. Nevertheless, such an emphasis is crucial within an understanding of the Spirit as the Spirit of God. The strange spirit which is God at work freeing people from what restricts and oppresses them will not be bound by human institutions. . . . God questions the rationality of human enterprise and the desire for order and control through the work of the Spirit in human affairs. Shirley can only experience her own release through the costly (and irrational) risk-taking of her flight to Greece and the challenge to the institutional structure of her own marriage through her brief encounter with Costas. Whether the specifics of her actions can be said to be 'the will of God' is open to question. But the work of the Spirit, as the Spirit of freedom, nevertheless presses her to break out of her present situation, as a direct result of her prayer and quest for relationship. On this understanding, the Spirit as the Spirit of freedom is none other than the redemptive Spirit of Christ, who rescues (saves) people from what constrains and crushes them. . . . It is often a dominant theme in films (*One Flew Over the Cuckoo's Nest*, *The Shawshank Redemption*) and frequently dealt with more darkly. In approaching Shirley Valentine from a pneumatological perspective, however, we are also suggesting where explorations of other films, whose focus is redemption/liberation, might usefully lead.

Clive Marsh and Gaye Ortiz
Explorations in Theology and Film

There was something we craved even more than mail – news of our missing comrades – especially news of those who had gone up-country on some work party and had not been heard of again. Were they still alive? How had they fared? The men in the ration parties made it their business to gather all the information they could and pass it on from one camp to the next. The minute they entered camp eager prisoners would surround them and pelt them with questions.

'Have ye heard anything of my mucker? Name of McIntosh. He was a sergeant in the in the Field Artillery – the 122nd. About middle-sized, he was. With dark brown hair. Expect he'd be wearing a beard.'

Usually the couriers shook their heads. Occasionally a name would give them a clue. Now and then the news was good; more often it was not.

Death was continuing to take its toll. The name uppermost for me was Dusty Miller's. Whenever an ox-cart appeared I was in the front rank of the questioners. I was looking forward to a reunion with Dusty and Dinty Moore. At every opportunity I asked visitors from other camps if they had any word. Time and again I put the same question and gave the descriptions. Repeatedly I received the same reply, 'Sorry chum, I don't remember anyone by that name – or of that description. Could you give me a clue?'

It was from one of the couriers that I learned how Dinty Moore had died. But there was still no word of Dusty. Then at last I met a prisoner who had been on the same work detail as him. 'Yes, I knew him,' he said. 'We were sent to Burma to cut a retreat route for the Japs. He was one of those left behind after the road was built to maintain it during the monsoon.'

'Where is he now?' I asked.

The man was reluctant to speak. He stammered for a minute or two. Then he replied, 'We had a pretty bad time of it. It was a repeat performance of the railway. And those who were left behind had an even harder time – especially after the Japs heard that defeat was possible.' He stopped.

'But what about Miller?' I asked again. The man looked away. 'The last news I had of him wasn't good.'

'What was it then?'

'According to what I heard, he was in trouble.'

'Dusty?'

'He got the Nip warrant officer in charge of his party down on him.'

'What had he done wrong?'

'That was it. He hadn't done anything wrong.' He

swallowed hard. 'The Nip hated him because he couldn't break him. You know how he was – a good man if ever there was one. That's why he hated him.'

'What did the Nip do to him?'

'He strung him up to a tree.'

I was aghast. 'You mean . . .' Then came the simple reply. 'Yes, he crucified him.' I could hardly speak. 'When?'

'About the beginning of August.'

'Just before the Japs . . .'

'Packed up, yes.' He turned away. He had said as much as he could bear to. I was so stunned that I didn't quite know what to do. I walked out from the group of chattering questioners in a daze.

Dusty dead? Dusty – the man of deep faith and warm heart – the man who was incapable of a mean act, even against a brutal tormentor. His goodness, it is true, had been recognised, not in sympathy, however, but in hate. Condemned by such radiant goodness, the warrant officer must have gone berserk.

There on that tree, like his Master, he died, so far from his homeland, so far from everyone, yet so near to God.

Ernest Gordon
Miracle on the River Kwai

133

Trinity Sunday

John 3:1-17

Ever [Jesus] has a way of penetrating to the essential meaning of Scripture, as . . . he exposes the deepest implications of God's ancient directives to his people.

John records in this Gospel lection that Nicodemus, a leading Pharisee, went to see Jesus one night and said to him, 'Master, we realise that you are a teacher who has come from God,' and began to ask some important questions that baffled him, even though he himself was a teacher of Israel. But instead of concentrating on their debate, let us remember that Jesus, like any teacher and scholar today, was also a great reader; and before he taught he read. Here is an extract from A. M. Hunter describing what Jesus read before he taught:

Robert Flint, once Professor of Divinity in Edinburgh University, used to tell his students that, if they would preach effectively, they must study both nature and human nature . . .

Sage counsel – so far as it goes. Yet Flint's prescription for study, as reported by one of his students, contains one notable omission. No student of the Gospels can fail to note that the greatest preacher of all read not in two books but in three – *The Book of Nature, The Book of Human Nature* and *The Book of the People of God.*

. . . To nature Jesus goes continually for illustrations of the will and ways of God. Best known perhaps is his, 'Consider the lilies of the field, how they grow'. For Jesus, these scarlet anemones which, because they grew so abundantly, the women used to fuel their kitchen stoves, were finer far than Solomon in all his glory. 'Today they are,' he said, 'and tomorrow they are not.' It is an old motif, this of the transience of life as seen in the fading flower, but Jesus gives it a new turn. His lesson is not, 'These perish, and so must we'. It is: 'God lavishes infinite pains on these, brief though their life is. How much more does he care for you his children!'

In the sunshine and the rain, falling on good and bad alike, he finds evidence of the grace of God. In the mystery of unfolding buds – first the green shoot, then the spike of corn, and then the full grain in the ear – he would have impatient men find an analogy of how the new divine force released in the world – the kingdom of God – grows irresistibly, inevitably, from seed time to harvest. A man sowing seed on a neighbouring hillside evokes from him a parable about the almighty sower and his harvest which, in spite of failures, exceeds all expectation. A shepherd's concern for a lost sheep furnishes him with a figure for his own work as the divine shepherd who goes seeking out and saving God's lost children. A hen with her chickens under her wings serves him as simile of how often he had sought – alas, in vain – to gather God's ancient people into his Father's kingdom.

Not that Jesus was blind to the terrible in nature. He saw the wolves that devour the flock, the vultures ever ready to swoop down on the carcass. He knew the earthquake and the flood that could sweep away a sand-built house like a cockle shell. Yet these things did not shadow his trust in the goodness of the great Father above. Everywhere in vivid, intense intimacy was the faith that this world, for all its evil and sin, was a room in his Father's house, and with it the kindliness of home.

Now consider the second book in which Jesus read deeply, as St John declares: '[Jesus] knew men so well, all of them, that he needed no evidence from others about a man, for he himself could tell what was in a man.' (John 2:25, NEB)

It has often been said that he was a great believer in men. Under no illusions about the evil in our human nature, he yet knew what by God's grace men might become. He who said that men were of 'more value than many sparrows' and that there was joy in heaven when a sinner repented, has rightly been credited with teaching the infinite value of the human soul in God's sight. Jesus had great faith in man – as witness his calling of twelve men, each, it has been said, capable of breaking his heart. He had, moreover, the faculty of discovering interest and worth in unlikely and unlovely people like the woman who was a sinner or the disreputable little inspector of taxes in Jericho. He was never interested in what class people belonged to but in who they were. He was concerned for them as real persons precious to God, potential members of his big family, and therefore to be pitied, and helped, and saved.

It is his parables, of course, which best show with what shrewd discerning eyes Jesus walked amid the human scene. The men and women in them are not puppets but real people, acting in character. Here, for instance, is a wealthy farmer, building still greater barns to house increasing crops, and dreaming of a carefree old age when, suddenly, he drops down dead; and here, at the other end of the scale, is a farm servant who, having done a hard day's work, must fall to and prepare his master's supper before he himself can 'get a bite'. Here, again, is a Sadducee, clad in purple and fine linen and 'faring sumptuously every day'; and there, at his gate, lies poor Lazarus, with his body festering with ulcers which the roaming street dogs rasp with their tongues.

. . . How unerringly too Jesus reads the characters of those people he encounters during his ministry! Jesus, says T. W. Manson, was never put off by pious humbugs but always brought them back to reality by the shortest possible route. Think of that first-century 'Holy Willie' called Simon (in Luke 7), type of all those 'good' people who (in Reinhold Niebuhr's phrase) 'do not know that they are not "good"'. Or that ostentatious 'lawyer' (in Luke 10) spoiling for a debate with Jesus about the law, when he asked, 'How can I love my neighbour when I don't know who he really is?' only to be answered, in a story about a hated Samaritan, 'Real love never asks questions like this. All it asks for is opportunities of going into action.' Or consider, finally, that 'theological inquisitive' (the breed is not yet extinct today) who asked Jesus if only a 'few' were going to be 'saved', only to be told in effect, 'It is a case of struggling, not of strolling into God's kingdom. Few enough, my friend, to make you afraid you may not be there. See to your entry!'

All these people in the parables – and how many more – are testimonies to Jesus' knowledge of man in his nobility and his nastiness, and demonstrate how deeply he had read the chequered *Book of Human Nature*.

We come, last, to the *Book of the People of God* – the Old Testament.

The Gospels reveal Christ's profound knowledge of his people's Scripture. He does not handle it like their professional theologians, the Scribes. Indeed, he accuses them of 'neglecting the commandment of God' in favour of 'the tradition of men' (Mark 7:8). He even criticises Moses' permission of divorce, calling it a concession to human hard-heartedness and pointing men back to God's primal intention in instituting marriage (Mark 10:2-9). Ever he has a way of penetrating to the essential meaning of Scripture, as in the Sermon on the Mount (Matthew 5:21-48) he exposes the deepest implications of God's ancient directives to his people.

Moreover, his thought naturally and instinctively clothes itself in scriptural phrase. His chosen name for himself – the Son of man – he probably took from Daniel 7. It is in words from the psalter and Isaiah that God speaks to him at his baptism. The story of his temptation he phrases – very significantly – in words describing old Israel's 'testing' in the wilderness. In the synagogue at Nazareth, after reading out Isaiah's prediction of the coming time of God's favour (Isaiah 61), he declares it to be fulfilled in his ministry. To John the Baptist's question from prison, 'Art thou he that cometh?', he replies in words recalling the promises in

Isaiah of God's future day of salvation. . . . By his entry into Jerusalem, his cleansing of the Temple and his words to his disciples at the Last Supper he makes explicit fulfilment of the prophets' (Zechariah and Jeremiah) anticipation in his own person. As in language recalling Hosea 6:2 he predicts his triumph over death (Mark 8:31) so he commits his spirit to God (Luke 23:46) with Psalm 31:5 upon his lips. Above all, in the prophecies of him whom we call 'Second Isaiah' he saw, as in a mirror, his own face and destiny, as the Suffering Servant of the Lord . . .

'Christ,' says P. T. Forsyth in a fine passage, 'used the Bible as a means of grace, not as a manual of Hebrew or other history. . . . He found in it the long purpose and deep scope of God's salvation. . . . He cared little for what our scholars expound . . . the religion of Israel. . . . What he found (in the Old Testament) was not the prophets' thoughts of God but God's invasion of them and their race by words and deeds of gracious power. . . . The torch he carried through the Old Testament was the Gospel of grace. . . . He read it with the eyes of faith . . . and he read it as a whole.'

A. M. Hunter
Jesus Lord and Saviour

Proper 4/Ordinary Time 9

Sunday between 29 May and 4 June inclusive (if after Trinity
Sunday)

Mark 2:23-3:6

*If you could
rewrite Sundays
the way you
want them to be,
where would you
draw the line?*

Intuition

The Pharisees were running a campaign to keep the Sabbath
special. Jesus fell foul of the way they thought the Sabbath
should really be kept. Their campaign to keep the Sabbath
special required people to desist from plucking corn. Their
campaign to keep the Sabbath special required people to
desist from non-emergency healings.

Now, if you could rewrite Sundays the way you want them
to be, where would you draw the line? Would you keep the
hospitals running just like any other day of the week, to get the
best return from expensive equipment and highly developed
operating theatres? Or would you try to assign a rest day to
a higher proportion of the staff?

If you could rewrite Sundays, would you keep the petrol
station open to refuel your car? Would you keep the corner
shop open to purchase your paper and the extra pint of milk?
Or would you want the staff in these places to benefit from
an extra day at home?

If you could rewrite Sundays, would you open the supermarket, the garden centre and the home improvement store,
so that much of the day-to-day business could go on undisturbed? Or would you want to signal that such activities are
disruptive of family life and religious sensitivities?

If you could rewrite Sundays, would you see an opportunity
for major sporting fixtures, to take the pressure off Saturday
and to provide families with something to do? Or would you
want to make sure that the churches were operating in a less
competitive marketplace?

Now, if you could rewrite Sundays the way you would
want them to be, where would you draw the line? What
provision would you like there to be?

Feeling

Now see how the whole thing looks to the man with the withered hand.

It must all have seemed so strange to the man with the withered hand. The hand had been like that for years. It had been like that on weekdays; it had been like that on Sabbaths. But never before had the withered hand caused so much controversy.

It must have seemed so strange to the man with the withered hand. Year in and year out he had longed to come face to face with a real healer who could have made that hand as good as new. But never before had he seen a real healer in that town.

. . . Sabbath by Sabbath he had been to that synagogue and no one had as much as noticed that he was there. But today he had been the centre of all attention. The Pharisees and Scribes had fixed their eyes on him from the moment he had walked in through the open door. Then Jesus had called him to step forward.

. . . He stood there on the very edge of being healed, waiting with excitement and expectation. But instead of being at the centre of miraculous healing, he stood at the heart of theological controversy.

It must have all seemed so strange to the man with the withered hand. All he heard was a simple command, 'Stretch out your hand'. All he did was to obey the command. He stretched out his hand and it was restored.

. . . As he returned home healed and restored, he heard the whispering conspiracy of the Pharisees. They were plotting to destroy the man who had healed him.

Now see how the whole thing looks to the man with the restored hand.

Leslie J. Francis
Personality Type and Scripture: Exploring Mark's Gospel

Proper 5/Ordinary Time 10

Sunday between 5 and 11 June inclusive (if after Trinity Sunday)

Mark 3:20-35

The light is there for those who will accept it, but if some refuse the light, where else can they hope to receive illumination?

The person who has committed the unpardonable sin figures powerfully in literature. There is, for example, Bunyan's man in the iron cage. There is the Welsh preacher Peter Williams, breaking the silence of night in George Borrow's *Lavengro* with his anguished cry: 'Pechod Ysprydd Glan! O Pechod, Ysprydd Glan!' (Oh, the sin against the Holy Spirit!) – which he was persuaded he had committed. Or there is Mr Paget , in Edmund Gosse's *Father and Son* who had thrown up his cure of souls because he became convinced that he had committed the sin against the Holy Ghost . . . 'Mr Paget was fond of talking, in private and in public, of his dreadful spiritual condition, and he would drop his voice while he spoke of having committed the Unpardonable Sin, with a sort of shuddering exultation, such as people sometimes feel in the possession of a very unusual disease. . . . Everybody longed to know what the exact nature had been of that sin against the Holy Ghost which had deprived Mr Paget of every glimmer of hope for time or for eternity. It was whispered that even my Father himself was not precisely acquainted with the character of it.' (E. Gosse: *Father and Son*)

Of course not, because the 'sin' existed only in Mr Paget's imagination. In real life there are few more distressing conditions calling for treatment by physicians of the soul than that of people who believe they have committed this sin. When they are offered the Gospel assurance of forgiveness for every sin, when they are reminded that 'the blood of Jesus . . . cleanses us from all sin' (1 John 1:7) they have a ready answer: there is one sin which forms an exception to this rule, and they have committed that sin; for it, in distinction from all other kinds of sin, there is no forgiveness. Did not our Lord himself say so? And they tend to become impatient when it is pointed out to them (quite truly) that the very fact of their concern over having committed it proves that they have not committed it.

What then did Jesus mean when he spoke in this way? His saying has been preserved in two forms. Luke records it as one of a series of sayings dealing with the Son of man or the Holy Spirit, but Mark gives it a narrative context . . .

According to Mark, Scribes or experts in the Jewish law

came down from Jerusalem to Galilee to assess the work which, as they heard, Jesus was doing there, and especially his ministry of exorcism – expelling demons from the lives of those who suffered under their domination. (This language indicates a real and sad condition, even if it would commonly be described in different terms today.) The Scribes came to a strange conclusion: 'He is possessed by Beelzebub, and by the prince of demons he casts out demons' (Mark 3:22). Beelzebub had once been the name of a Canaanite divinity, 'the Lord of the high place,' but by this time it was used by Jews to denote the ruler of the abyss, the abode of demons. When Jesus knew of this, he exposed the absurdity of supposing that Satan's power could be overthrown by Satan's aid. Then he went on to charge those who had voiced this absurd conclusion with blaspheming against the Holy Spirit. Why? Because they deliberately ascribed the Holy Spirit's activity to demonic agency.

For every kind of sin, then, for every form of blasphemy or slander, it is implied that forgiveness is available – presumably when the sin is repented of. But what if one were to repent of blasphemy against the Holy Spirit? Is there no forgiveness for the person who repents of this sin?

The answer seems to be that the nature of this sin is such that one does not repent of it, because those who commit it and persist in it do not know that they are sinning. Mark tells his readers why Jesus charged those Scribes with blaspheming against the Holy Spirit: it was because 'they had said, "He has an unclean spirit"' (Mark 3:30). Jesus was proclaiming the kingly rule of God, and his bringing relief to soul-sick demon-possessed mortals was a token that the kingly rule of God was present and active in his ministry. 'If it is by the finger of God that I cast out demons,' he said, 'then the kingdom of God has come upon you.' (Luke 11:20; in Matthew 12:28 where these words also appear, 'finger of God' is replaced by 'Spirit of God'.) If some people looked at the relief which he was bringing to the bodies and minds of men and women and maintained that he was doing so with the help of their great spiritual oppressor, the prince of demons, then their eyes were so tightly closed to the light that for them light had become darkness and good had become evil. The light is there for those who will accept it, but if some refuse the light, where else can they hope to receive illumination?

[Luke] places the saying about blaspheming the Holy Spirit between a saying about the Spirit's heavenly role as counsel for the defence of those who confess the Son of man (that is, Jesus) and a saying about the Spirit's enabling confessors of

Jesus before an earthly tribunal to say the right words at the right time. In this context a different emphasis is given to the matter of blasphemy against the Spirit from that given to it by Mark. It is suggested by Luke that the blaspheming of the Spirit involves a refusal of his powerful help when it is available to save the disciples of Jesus from denying him and so committing apostasy. If so, blasphemy against the Spirit in this context is tantamount to apostasy, the deliberate and decisive repudiation of Jesus as Lord. This is not the only New Testament passage which warns against the irremediable evil of apostasy: another well known example is Hebrews 6:4-6, where it is said to be impossible to renew apostates to repentance, since they have repudiated the only way of salvation.

. . . In Mark's context, then, the sin against the Holy Spirit involves deliberately shutting one's eyes to the light and consequently calling good evil; in Luke . . . it is irretrievable apostasy.

F. F. Bruce
The Hard Sayings of Jesus

Proper 6/Ordinary Time 11

Sunday between 12 and 18 June inclusive (if after Trinity Sunday)

Mark 4:26-34

Because the subject matter is the mystery of the kingdom, the listener should expect snatches of insight and partial discoveries rather than mastery of the subject matter.

All the lections for today register transitions of one type or another: historical, political, theological or personal. The old comes to an end; something new is beginning. Our Gospel is no exception; Mark presents that 'something new' as the kingdom, and he does so in parables about seed.

[First,] parables are not simple little stories used by Jesus so that everyone within the sound of his voice could understand his teaching. On the contrary, not everyone did understand, even though Jesus' offer was to anyone who had ears to hear (Mark 4:9, 23).

Second, parables are a form of literature that, like poetry, demand a great deal from the listener. They are not obvious to all and sundry, to every casual passer-by who may or may not make any personal investment in Jesus or the kingdom. Parables, then, have a revealing-concealing quality, creating their own hearers and non-hearers.

Third, those who do hear are an inner circle, not of superior intelligence but of personal attachment to Jesus. They are 'with Jesus'. But even for these, understanding is not easy, even with Jesus' further instruction. As the interpretation of the parable of the sower illustrates (Mark 4:14-20), the explanation can be as difficult to grasp as the parable itself. But the point is, understanding is linked to one's relation to Jesus.

Fourth, the use of parables by Jesus is not surprising because Jesus was himself a parable of God. Jesus as the presence of God, as the Son of God, was not obviously so to everyone. He spoke of himself as the lamp; he spoke of light and shadow, of the revealed and the hidden (Mark 4:21-25). Only intentional, intense giving of oneself to him and his message is fruitful.

And finally, because the subject matter is the mystery of the kingdom, the listener should expect snatches of insight and partial discoveries rather than mastery of the subject matter.

And what do the two parables say of the kingdom? The parable of the seed growing secretly (verses 26-29) . . . has been interpreted from two perspectives. If verse 29 is the key, then the parable says that now is the time to reap the harvest;

this is the end time; all that has gone before was but the growing season. More likely, however, is the interpretation that focuses more upon the growth that takes place totally apart from human effort (the sower sleeps and rises) and from human understanding ('he does not know how'). The seed carries its own future in its bosom, and efforts to coerce and force growth are futile. The kingdom of God is exactly that – the kingdom *of* God. The thought both chastens and encourages followers of Jesus.

The parable of the mustard seed (verses 30-32) is clearly a word of encouragement. Let those concerned, frustrated, or even depressed by small beginnings, by the apparent insignificance of the enterprise to which life and resources are committed, take heart. Let the vision of the end ('the greatest of all shrubs') inspire and inform today's effort, knowing all the while that the end as well as the beginning are God's doing and not our own.

Fred B. Craddock
Preaching Through the Christian Year: 'B'

Proper 7/Ordinary Time 12

Sunday between 19 and 25 June inclusive (if after Trinity Sunday)

Mark 4:35-41

How can faith address fear in today's world?

In January 1736, John Wesley was on his way by ship to Georgia in the United States where he hoped to preach the Gospel in the New World.

On the voyage his ship met with some violent storms. Having survived one, Wesley records in his journal for Friday, 23 January:

'In the evening another storm began. In the morning it increased so that they were forced to let the ship drive. I could not but say to myself, "How is it that thou hast no faith?" being still unwilling to die. About one in the afternoon, almost as soon as I had stepped out of the great cabin door, the sea did not break as usual, but came with a full, smooth tide over the side of the ship. I was vaulted over with the water in a moment, and so stunned that I scarce expected to lift my head up again till the sea should give up her dead. But, thanks be to God, I received no hurt at all. About midnight the storm ceased.

Sunday 25.

'At noon our third storm began. At four it was more violent than any we had had before. Now, indeed, we could say, "The waves of the sea were mighty, and raged horribly. They rose up to the heavens above, and clave down to hell beneath." The winds roared round about us, and – what I never heard before – whistled as distinctly as if it had been a human voice. The ship not only rocked to and fro with the utmost violence, but shook and jarred with so unequal, grating a motion, that one could not but with great difficulty keep one's hold of anything, nor stand a moment without it. Every ten minutes came a shock against the stern or side of the ship, which one would think would dash the planks in a thousand pieces. In the height of the storm, a child, privately baptised before, was brought to be (publicly) received into the church. It put me in mind of Jeremiah's buying the field when the Chaldeans were on the point of destroying Jerusalem, and seemed a pledge of the mercy God designed to show us, even in the land of the living.

'We spent two or three hours after prayers in conversing

suitably to the occasion, confirming one another in a calm submission to the wise, holy, gracious will of God. And now a storm did not appear so terrible as before. Blessed be the God of all consolation, who alone doeth wonders, and is able to deliver his people.'

Part of a footnote concerning the storm of Sunday 25 January says: 'The diary notes, and to some extent the account itself, were written during the storms. The handwriting on this page shakes with the shaking of the ship . . .'

The student who traces the sequence of events will see that the storm was one of the crucial events in the history of early Methodism. It shook the nerve of all on board, passengers and seamen – of all except the Moravians. It was their great peacefulness when the sea split the mainsail, and the joy of their singing, that brought Wesley's incipient friendship to maturity. . . . One cannot resist the conviction that when, about a year later, in Georgia, Wesley translated and reversified Rothe's great hymn, he recalled the Moravians and the storm, and the unshaken trust that enabled the exiles to sing, amidst the 'roaring of the wind' and the terrible 'screaming' of the English, their psalm on the power of God: 'Though waves and storms go o'er my head.' What psalm did the Moravians sing at their evening worship on that memorable Sunday?

The Journal of John Wesley: Volume 1

The great themes of the Christian tradition permeate this narrative: the theme of faith and the theme of fear. Jesus said to the disciples, 'Why are you afraid? Have you still no faith?' But how can faith address fear in today's world?

Take the example of the young child who fears the dark. There she lies imprisoned in her bed, desperately trying to make sense of a confusing and irrational world. Monsters lurk in the cupboard; fiends dwell under the bed. How can faith address the young child's fear of the dark?

Take the example of the adolescent youth who fears the empty streets. There he hides in prison behind his door, desperately trying to avoid the intimidation and conflict of a hostile world. Gangs lurk round the corner; terrorists dwell in the shadows. How can faith address the adolescent youth's fear of the empty streets?

Take the example of the young adult who fears some crippling illness. There she lies imprisoned within her anxiety, desperately trying to identify and diagnose the symptoms of physical disease. Cancers lurk under every cell. Viruses dwell in every organ. How can faith address the young adult who fears some crippling illness?

Take the example of the middle-aged executive who fears the empty desk. There she works imprisoned by the company, desperately trying to identify the forces for reorganisation and rationalisation. Take-overs lurk behind every board meeting; redundancies dwell in every restructuring. How can faith address the middle-aged executive who fears the empty desk?

Take the example of the frail pensioner who fears the hour of death. There he survives, imprisoned within the body he dreads to leave, desperately trying to face the certainty of mortality and to embrace the uncertainty of immortality. Black-clothed undertakers lurk in the shadows; long-faced ministers dwell in the attics. How can faith address the frail pensioner who fears the hour of death?

Leslie J. Francis
Personality Type and Scripture: Exploring Mark's Gospel

Proper 8/Ordinary Time 13

Sunday between 26 June and 2 July inclusive

Mark 5:21-43

*Nothing is certain.
. . . Everything is
a matter of faith.*

Eleven months have passed since the cancer in my body was first detected – eleven months of the limited life I am expected to have left, the original sentence being about one year. The medical prognosis is still the same, and the latest scan showed a further increase in the tumour. The future officially is bleak, and I am getting used to people looking at me as a dying man under sentence of death. Nothing is certain. I'm not out of the wood yet. Everything is a matter of faith . . .

The opposite to faith is fear, and I have found that there is a constant running battle between the two. In one sense, fear is faith in what you do not want to happen. Job once said, 'The thing I fear comes upon me, and what I dread befalls me' (3:25). There is a powerful truth in that statement. When we are afraid of something, we almost pre-condition it to happen. Our fears, however unfounded and irrational they may be, can trigger the fulfilment of those fears.

Fear has been described as the greatest threat to health in our generation, simply because fear is so widespread. Fear is a great deceiver and destroyer. It robs our minds of peace; it breaks our relationships; it ruins our health; it goads us into foolish, impulsive and sometimes violent action; it paralyses our thinking, trusting and loving . . .

God never promises to protect us from problems, only to help us in them. If we leave God out of the picture, those difficulties might so strip away our sense of security that we feel vulnerable, anxious and afraid. On the other hand, those same difficulties could drive us back to God and so strengthen our faith. We might feel just as vulnerable, but we *have* to trust God because there really is no alternative; and then we discover that God is with us in the dark as in the light, in pain as in joy. When I was going through a traumatic time in my life, a friend of mine said, 'You cannot trust God too much.'

David Watson
Fear No Evil: A Personal Struggle with Cancer

Proper 9/Ordinary Time 14

Sunday between 3 and 9 July inclusive

Mark 6:1-13

Unsure of his status at home?

A writer – as well as a prophet – without honour?

Years of struggling had not made him (Hans Christian Anderson) either sour or aggressive, but they had left their mark upon him, so that even after his fame had spread all over Europe and beyond, he still felt unsure of his status at home.

In 1843, after a bad review of his *Agnete and the Merman*, a play of his, Hans Anderson wrote to a friend, Henriette Wulff: 'May I never see that homeland which has eyes for my faults but no heart for the greatness God has deposited in me . . . As always, the icy blasts come from Denmark and turn me to stone in this foreign land.' (Written from France.)

Monica Stirling
The Wild Swan

As James Cone has put it, 'Sin for blacks is loss of identity'. This theme can be seen not only in contemporary African American literature but also in the autobiographical narratives of ex-slaves and in spirituals. The forgiveness that the nineteenth century slave 'Old Elizabeth' receives from her encounter with Jesus bestows not a sense of unworthiness but rather 'somebodiness'. Elizabeth's memoir, narrated orally in her ninety-seventh year, includes on its title page the baptism affirmation of Galatians: 'There is neither Jew nor Greek, there is neither bond nor free, there is neither male nor female, for ye are all one in Jesus Christ.' Elizabeth was born in Maryland in 1766 to slave parents. She was separated from her parents at age ten and became so lonely that she escaped from her new master to find her mother. When she was discovered and was about to be separated once again from her family, her mother indicated that she had 'nobody in the wide world to look to but God'. This did not console Elizabeth;

indeed, she notes that 'these words fell upon my heart with ponderous weight, and seemed to add to my grief'.

The theme of heaviness, of a burden too great to bear, is found in many narratives of people who have suffered. Elizabeth's burden is a lost identity, a dehumanised and dehumanising condition. But Elizabeth, whose parents were religious and belonged to the Methodist Society, does not allow this burden to overwhelm her. Indeed, 'I betook myself to prayer, and in every lonely place I found an altar. I mourned sore like a dove and chattered forth my sorrow, moaning in the corners of the field, and under the fences.' She weeps like this for six months and eventually finds herself in despair. She identifies herself as a sinner, unfit to be in the presence of God. But then she hears a voice telling her to 'rise up and pray'; that voice gives her strength.

She says, 'I fell on my knees and prayed the best I could the Lord's Prayer. Knowing no more to say, I halted, but continued on my knees. My spirit was then *taught* to pray, "Lord, have mercy on me – Christ save me". Immediately there appeared a director, clothed in white raiment. I thought he took me by the hand and said, "Come with me".' She embarks upon a long journey that ends up at a fiery gulf, and she assumes that her hope in being saved was 'no more than a hair; still, pray, and it will be sufficient.' She renews her struggle, and finds that every cry for mercy and salvation raises her higher and higher. She then sees 'the Saviour with his hand stretched out to receive me. An indescribably glorious light was *in* him, and he said, "Peace, peace, come to me." At this moment I felt that my sins were forgiven me, and the time of my deliverance was at hand.'

Elizabeth describes this forgiveness in terms of being filled with 'light and love'. Immediately thereafter, however, she is also given a mission – even though she is not yet thirteen years old. As she narrates it, 'Immediately a light fell upon my head, and I was filled with light, and I was shown the world lying in wickedness, and was told I must go there, and call people to repentance, for the day of the Lord was at hand; and this message was a heavy yoke upon me, so that I wept bitterly at the thought of what I should have to pass through. While I wept I heard a voice say, "Weep not, some will laugh at thee, some will scoff at thee, and the dogs will bark at thee, but while thou doest my will, I will be with thee to the ends of the earth."' The next day, Elizabeth says, 'I had come to myself, I felt like a new creature in Christ, and all my desire was to see the Saviour'. Elizabeth receives a transformative forgiveness in her encounter with Jesus. Not only is she given a sense of identity, of 'somebodiness', but she also receives a mission to call people to repentance. She will continue to struggle to appropriate that forgiveness, both because of the appallingly dehumanising conditions of slavery (she was not freed until she was thirty, and the effects would linger throughout her life) and because of the resistance she encounters as a woman, particularly a black woman, proclaiming and embodying the Gospel in PROPHETIC (my capitals) terms. But she receives aid in that struggle from the Holy Spirit, who she frequently invokes in her memoir, the Spirit who guides, judges and consoles her as she perseveres as a forgiven and forgiving messenger of the Gospel . . .

It is regrettable, however, that neither the Church in her time nor in our own has been able to take the time not only to listen to Elizabeth's testimony, but to hear it as a prophetic judgement.

The rhythms of Elizabeth's memoir are found also in African American spirituals. The spirituals are filled with laments concerning the people's suffering, but ultimately they affirm the people's hope that God is enabling a better future. That hope is both personal, as in the affirmation that there is a 'balm in Gilead' that can heal the 'sin-sick soul', and social, as in *Go down, Moses* and the call to *Steal Away to Jesus*. Or, more sharply put, the spirituals as a whole embrace both personal and social hope for a future not determined by the past, a hope that requires a prophetic denunciation of the suffering and oppression found in the present. Further, the spirituals also recognise the importance of personal accountability and the priority of forgiven-ness to forgiving, seen in such spirituals as *Standing in the Need of Prayer*.

L. Gregory Jones
Embodying Forgiveness

151

Proper 10/Ordinary Time 15

Sunday between 10 and 16 July inclusive

Mark 6:14-29

*Success versus
significance.*

One way to read [this] passage, then, is in terms of success versus significance. Success, as the world measures it, is seen in the court of Herod. There we find the chief of state and his advisers, the military commanders, the leading people of the country; they are the ones who can afford leisure and pleasure; they can get what they want when they want it. John the Baptist, alone in his cell, doomed and helpless to save his life, appears in shocking contrast to the glitter of the successful people of his time. Our minds are perpetually and perversely fascinated by the wealth, power and intrigue of Herod's court; yet the significance of the text lies in the death of that starkly simple prophet in Herod's prison. The Gospel here invites us to look closely at success . . . and then choose significance as we follow Jesus on his way.

Lamar Williamson, Jun.
Mark: Interpretation Series of Commentaries

Put on your villain's crown and explore the story from Herod's perspective.

Put on your villain's crown and listen to John's accusation, to John's incisive indictment of your behaviour. Watch John look you in the eye and hear John proclaim, 'It is not lawful for you to have your brother's wife'. What powerful ruler would tolerate such impertinence?

Put on your villain's crown and send your men to arrest John, to confine John to your prison cell. Watch John languish in the prison darkness and hear John's solitary and plaintive cry. What powerful ruler could resist such proper retribution?

Put on your villain's crown and summons John to proclaim his message, to preach his Gospel of righteousness. Hear John's passion for truth, watch his unflinching grasp on integrity. What powerful ruler could fail to be moved by such obvious signs of righteousness and of holiness?

Put on your villain's crown and watch the young girl dance. Let your eyes and your heart be seduced by the young girl's grace and guile. What powerful ruler could reward such display with anything less than a lavish reward?

Put on your villain's crown and feel your heart torn asunder by the young girl's request. Let your eyes survey the crowd who witnessed your promise on oath. Let your mind evaluate the options. What powerful ruler could fail to recognise when he has been caught in such an obvious trap?

Put on your villain's crown and command the executioner to act. Let your eyes rest on the platter. Let your mind dwell on the severed head. What powerful ruler could fail to be conscious of his awesome power over life and limb?

Put on your villain's crown and live with the consequences of your act. Let your sleeping hours be haunted with the nightmares of the execution. Let your waking hours be haunted with the fears of John brought back to life. What powerful ruler could obliterate the memory of his guilt?

Put on your villain's crown and explore the story from Herod's perspective.

Leslie J. Francis
Personality Type and Scripture: Exploring Mark's Gospel

Proper 11/Ordinary Time 16

Sunday between 17 and 23 July inclusive

Mark 6:30-34, 53-56

All of life belongs to God and all brokenness awaits healing.

The idea behind inner healing is simply that we can ask Jesus Christ to walk back to the time we were hurt and to free us from the effects of that wound in the present. This involves two things then:

- bringing to light the things that have hurt us. Usually this is best done with another person; even the talking out of the problem is in itself a healing process.

- praying the Lord to heal the binding effects of the hurtful incidents of the past. Jesus, as Lord of time, is able to do what we cannot: he can heal those wounds of the past that still cause us suffering.

The most I was ever able to do as a counsellor was to help the person bring to the foreground of consciousness the things that were buried in the past, so that they could consciously cope with them in the present. Now I am discovering that the Lord can heal these wounds – sometimes immediately – and can bring the counselling process to its completion in a deep healing.

At times, these hurts may seem slight to an adult mind, but we must be sensitive to see things as a child would. I remember once praying for a woman whose complaint was that her inner life was always bleak and boring, even though her professional life was in itself full and exciting. When we finally found out what had caused her to shut off the flow of life it was an incident that happened when she was ten years old.

Francis MacNutt
Healing

Reconciling love is patient and persevering, for its ministry is daily, routine, never-ending. It is riddled with complications and complexities. It takes an enduring hope to tutor in a drug-rehabilitation centre, to visit people in prison, to pray for judges and lawmakers and corporation executives. The disciple comes soon to acknowledge that his or her own limits and frailty prepare the ground for forgiveness and acceptance of others.

Reconciliation is a responsibility that we cannot delegate. Each of us is part of a pattern of relationships that demand respect and non-violence. Our spirit will be tested at critical moments: when the funds for our poverty project are cut; when someone else is awarded the honour we deserve; when we are shunned or rejected; and by the wearying tasks of maintaining an honest, caring, community. 'While we live we are constantly being delivered to death for Jesus' sake, so that the life of Jesus may be revealed in our mortal flesh' (2 Corinthians 4:11).

The ministry of reconciliation has no defined or definable limits. All of life belongs to God and all brokenness awaits healing: distorted and destructive political systems, damaged personal relationships of all manner and making, our own failed covenants with ourselves and with God. Healing is needed in the caste systems of India, the capitalist systems of the West, the places where patriarchalism and militarism stunt life and where people suffer the consequences of greed and oppression. Healing is needed in the delicate systems of renewal and rebirth within our larger sacred community, the earth. The wounds of broken-hearted mothers, marginalised Indians, excommunicated mavericks cry for healing, as do those of isolated and alienated psyches and spirits starved for dignity and affection.

Joan Puls OSF
Hearts Set on the Pilgrimage: In Search of a Common Spirituality

Proper 12/Ordinary Time 17

Sunday between 24 and 30 July inclusive

John 6:1-21

Jesus knew what he was going to do, that he would perform a sign providing something qualitatively better than what was expected.

Because John has no account of a eucharistic Last Supper many commentators say that his account of the Feeding of the Five Thousand is his theological equivalent. Phrases such as 'he took', 'he gave thanks', appear in the Synoptic Gospels and in this account in John. Here is one of my favourite pieces concerning Holy Communion or the Eucharist:

Was ever another command so obeyed? For century after century, spreading slowly to every continent and country and among every race on earth, this action has been done, in every conceivable human circumstance, for every conceivable human need from infancy and before it to extreme old age and after it, from pinnacles of earthly greatness to the refuge of fugitives in the caves and dens of the earth.

Men have found no better thing than this to do for kings at their crowning and for criminals going to the scaffold; for armies in triumph or for a bride and bridegroom in a little country church; for the proclamation of a dogma or for a good crop of wheat; for the wisdom of the parliament of a mighty nation or for a sick old woman afraid to die; for a schoolboy sitting an examination or for Columbus setting out to discover America; for the famine of whole provinces or for the soul of a dead lover; in thankfulness because my father did not die of pneumonia; for a village headman much tempted to return to fetish because the yams had failed; because the Turk was at the gates of Vienna; for the settlement of a strike; for a son for a barren woman; for Captain So-and-so, wounded and prisoner of war; while the lions roared in the nearby amphitheatre; on the beach at Dunkirk; while the hiss of scythes in the thick June grass came faintly through the windows of the church; tremulously, by an old monk on the fiftieth anniversary of his vows; furtively, by an ex-bishop who had hewn timber all day in a prison camp near Murmansk; gorgeously for the canonisation of St Joan of Arc – one could fill many pages with the reasons why people have done this, and not tell a hundredth part of them.

And best of all, week by week and month by month, on a hundred thousand successive Sundays, faithfully, unfailingly across all the parishes of Christendom, the pastors have done just this to make the *plebs sancta Dei* – the holy common people of God.

Dom Gregory Dix
The Shape of the Liturgy

That the feeding occurs at Passover is important for the writer. At Passover, Jesus cleansed the Temple and spoke of his approaching death (John 2). At Passover, Jesus had a meal with his disciples in Jerusalem and spoke of his approaching death (John 13). In the account before us the feeding will not only be told in eucharistic language (John 6:11, 23), but it will be followed by a discourse on the life-giving flesh and blood of Jesus (John 6:51-59). We have, then, a story that has significance beyond that of Jesus' compassion on hungry crowds. In fact, verses 5-6 make it abundantly clear that Jesus knew what he was going to do, that he would perform a sign providing something qualitatively better than what was expected. The preacher would do well not to reach back into the Synoptic Gospels to pick up the 'compassion on the hungry' theme. Jesus feeds the people, to be sure, but the reader has already been alerted to look beyond the bread to the Bread. This is no isolated format in John; many of the stories are so developed. Jesus' mother wanted him to provide wine for wedding guests, and Jesus performed a revelatory sign beyond the expectation of Mary (John 2). Martha and Mary wanted a deceased brother, and Jesus responded in a way beyond resuscitating a corpse to offering resurrection and life to the world (John 11). To preach on John 6:1-21 is to open the door to a ministry of Jesus beyond the immediate wants and expectations of those who seek what he can give.

Fred B. Craddock
Preaching Through The Christian Year: 'B'

Proper 13/Ordinary Time 18

Sunday between 31 July and 6 August inclusive

John 6:24-35

A common meal is always more than a matter of satisfying the appetites of the individuals who partake of it.

Many people see things entirely from a selfish viewpoint. Karel Capek, a Czech writer, imagined the reactions of a baker, living in the time of Jesus, after Jesus had performed the miracle of feeding the five thousand.

The Five Loaves

'You know, neighbour, no baker can put up with that; how could he? If it became the custom for anyone who liked to feed five thousand people with five loaves and two small fishes, what would become of the bakers, tell me that? It doesn't matter so much about the fishes; they grow themselves in the water and anyone who likes can catch them. But a baker must buy flour and firewood at a high price, he must employ an assistant and pay him wages; he must keep a shop, he must pay taxes, and this, and that, and by the time he's finished, he's glad if he has a few ha'pence left over for himself so that he needn't go begging. And he – he just looks up to heaven and has enough bread for five or I don't know how many thousand people; the flour doesn't cost him anything, he doesn't have to have wood carried long distances, no expenses, no work – well, of course he can give the people bread for nothing.

And he never thinks how he's depriving the bakers in the neighbourhood of their hard-earned profits! I tell you it's unfair competition and he ought to be prevented from doing it.'

Karel Capek
Source unknown

Normally, we eat in order to relieve our hunger and provide our bodies and minds with energy for our work: but sometimes we are invited to a meal which has a further meaning to it. For example, we attend in order to celebrate an anniversary, to pay tribute to a person's service or to raise money for a good cause.

These men were sharing a meal with Jesus – that is the significant fact. In many parts of Asia today, a common meal is always more than a matter of satisfying the appetites of the individuals who partake of it. It is a way of expressing a very close association between them. This was certainly so in Palestine in the time of Jesus. Why the scandalised cries from the doctors of the law when Jesus and his disciples sat down to a meal in 'bad company' in Levi's house? Simply because by this act, Jesus was publicly identifying himself with a stratum of society which was totally unacceptable to the respectable representatives of institutional religion. 'He actually *eats* with tax gatherers and sinners!' they cried. When Jewish Christians in Jerusalem accused Peter of 'sitting at table' with Gentiles, they were similarly scandalised.

. . . In effect Jesus is saying, 'You have kept company with me over these past months. You have seen me at work and listened to my words. I have spent time alone with you interpreting the meaning of my ministry. You have marked my way of dealing with evil. The inevitable outcome of this now looms over us in the shape of the cross. In sharing this meal with me you are identifying yourselves completely with me in the ministry. You pledge yourselves to embody, proclaim and impart my love in a continuing fellowship of reconciliation and healing.' Thus they become 'the body of Christ'.

Brian A Greet
To Communion – with Confidence

The problem with miracles is that we tend to get mesmerised by them, focusing on God's responsibility and forgetting our own. Miracles let us off the hook. They appeal to the part of us that is all too happy to let God feed the crowd, save the world, do it all. We do not have what it takes, after all. What we have to offer is not enough to make any difference at all, so we hold back and wait for a miracle, looking after our own needs and looking for God to help those who cannot help themselves.

Sitting in the crowd, waiting for God to act, we can hang on to our own little loaves of bread. They are not much; they would not go far. Besides, if Jesus is in charge of the bread, doesn't that excuse us from sharing our own? God will provide, let God provide. 'Send the crowds away to go into the villages,' the disciples say, 'and buy food for themselves.'

'They need not go away,' Jesus says, 'you give them something to eat.' Not me but you; not my bread but yours; not sometime or somewhere else but right here and now. Stop looking for someone else to solve the problem and solve it yourselves. Stop waiting for food to fall from the sky and share what you have. Stop waiting for a miracle and participate in one instead.

Bring what you have to me; that is where to begin. Remember that there is no such thing as 'your' bread or 'my' bread, only 'our' bread, as in 'give us this day our daily bread'. However much you have, just bring it to me and believe that it is enough to begin with, enough to get the ball rolling, enough to start a trend. Be the first in the crowd to turn your pockets inside out; be the first on your block to start a miracle.

No one knows how it really happened. Your guess is as good as mine, but what Jesus has been saying to his followers forever he goes on saying today: 'They need not go away; you give them something to eat.' If it is a saying that strikes fear in our hearts, that makes the loaves we have seem like nothing at all, we have only to remember what he says next: 'Bring them to me.' Amen.

Barbara Brown Taylor
The Seeds of Heaven

Proper 14/Ordinary Time 19

Sunday between 7 and 13 August inclusive

John 6:35, 41-51

What Jesus knew beyond a shadow of a doubt was that wherever there was plenty of God there would be plenty of everything else.

Each of the four Gospel writers records the life of Jesus in a different way. Picking and choosing from all the stories they knew about what their Lord said and did, each of them came up with a different combination. Only Matthew and Luke write about Jesus' birth, for instance, while John is the only one who tells the story of Lazarus being raised from the dead. The Sermon on the Mount is found only in Matthew, and while Luke includes about half of the same sermon in his Gospel, he says that it took place on a wide plain.

But one thing that all four writers included in their Gospels is the story about the miraculous feeding of the five thousand. It was too important a story to leave out – too important in the life of Jesus and too important in the life of the church. It was a story about Jesus' ability to provide for their needs, and not only for their spiritual needs but for their human needs as well. When they were sick, Jesus healed them; when they were sad, Jesus blessed them; when they were hungry, Jesus fed them.

In time, it became a story that early Christians told around the table when they gathered for worship. As they blessed, broke and shared the miraculous bread of the Lord's Supper, they remembered that other time when bread was miraculously blessed, broken and shared, and it was as if Jesus stood among them again, laying his hands on a little so that it became enough for all.

The feeding of the five thousand is a story that carries echoes of other stories, like the Old Testament story about how manna fell from the sky to feed the children of Israel in the wilderness. That was the first bread miracle that God worked on their behalf. They were far away from home in that story too, without a clue where their next meal would come from, when God sent manna from heaven to fill their bellies and feed their trust in him. In the second book of Kings, you can read the story of another bread miracle in which the prophet Elisha fed a hundred hungry men with twenty barley loaves. His disciples protested that it was not enough to set before all those people, but Elisha insisted and the Lord provided, so that everyone ate his fill and there were leftovers besides.

So this miracle story is one in a series of bread miracles in the Bible, and an impressive one at that. Jesus feeds five thousand men, Matthew tells us, not counting the women and children who are present. He feeds what amounts to a small town with five loaves and two fishes, a meal that multiplies until no one can eat any more and the scraps fill twelve baskets. It is a miracle, and perhaps that should be the end of that, but miracles tend to nag at those of us who do not experience them very often.

We tend to wonder at things, like how did it happen exactly? Did Jesus multiply the loaves all at once, so that the disciples had to recruit people to help them carry all that bread? Or did it happen as the loaves were being passed through the crowd? When someone tore off a chunk of bread, did the loaf suddenly grow? As you reached out to take the loaf, did it sort of jump into your hand and get bigger? Or did new loaves appear while no one was looking? Maybe you set yours down for a moment as you shifted your child from one arm to the other, and when you reached down to pick it up again there were two loaves instead of one? How did it happen exactly?

Matthew does not tell us. What he does tell us is that the miracle happened at 'a lonely place apart', which was where Jesus had gone after he heard the news that John the Baptist was dead, beheaded at the whim of a dancing girl. Having heard that, he wanted to be alone, and who could blame him? . . .

He may have needed to be alone, but the crowd had needs of their own. They were sick, they were sad, they were hungry, and while anyone but the Son of God might have ordered them to get lost, Jesus had compassion on them. His heart went out to them and he spent the afternoon walking among them, laying his hands on them and saying the things they needed to hear.

When evening fell, the disciples found him and suggested that he send everyone away to buy supper in one of the nearby villages. They meant no harm; they were simply being practical . . .

'They need not go away,' Jesus said to his disciples, 'you give them something to eat.' I wish I had been there. I wish I could have seen how they looked at each other when he said that. Give them something to eat? Us? You are in charge here, Jesus; you are the boss. What do you mean, *we* should give them something to eat? All we have between us is five loaves and two salted fishes, which is hardly a snack for twelve men, never mind five thousand. There are *five thousand people* out there, Jesus. No disrespect intended, but you are not making sense.

He may not have been making sense, but then again he may have had a sense of the situation that went beyond the disciples' common sense. They were, after all, operating out of a sense of scarcity. They looked at the crowd, saw no picnic baskets or backpacks, and assumed that no one had anything to eat. They looked at their own meagre resources and assumed that it was not enough to go around their own circle, much less to feed the whole crowd.

But Jesus operated on a different set of assumptions. If the disciples operated out of a sense of scarcity, then what Jesus operated out of was a sense of plenty. He looked at the same things the disciples looked at, but where they saw not enough, he saw plenty: plenty of time, plenty of food, and plenty of possibilities with the resources at hand. Not that he knew how it was all going to work out exactly – he was human, remember, as well as divine – but what Jesus knew beyond a shadow of a doubt was that wherever there was plenty of God there would be plenty of everything else.

Barbara Brown Taylor
The Seeds of Heaven

What is the content of the message of miracles? Often we are fascinated with miracles because they appear to be demonstrations of raw, naked, and unambiguous power. A reversal of the natural order is a demonstration of power, and we are interested in Jesus and his miracles, at least in the first instance, insofar as they demonstrate for us the uses of power. To heal the sick, as with the lame or the blind or the woman with the haemorrhage of blood, demonstrates power to do the right and good thing. The first miracle that Jesus wrought, at the marriage feast of Cana in Galilee, demonstrates a power to bring order out of chaos, but the essence of a miracle is not in its power, nor in its extraordinary capacity, nor in its ability to attract attention and high-visibility, but rather in its capacity to meet and to satisfy a need. A miracle is a response to what is most needed; it is, at heart, not a demonstration of power but an answer to prayer. In the feeding of the five thousand the immediate need of the crowd was met and satisfied by the wondrous extension of the loaves and fishes, but that was

163

not the miracle. The miracle was that in this the people saw 'the prophet who is to come into the world'. Their eyes were opened and they saw Jesus as he was: God's message to the world.

There is always a great temptation to spiritualise this story, to see the loaves and fishes and the feeding of the crowd as mere metaphors for the kind of spiritual refreshment that Jesus offers his people, and there is some warrant for reducing the food services aspect of this story. Jesus himself warns the people that they should not go after the bread that perishes and spoils, like the manna of the Exodus, but should seek 'the food which endures to eternal life, which the Son of Man will give to you'. He goes on to say, in John 6:33 and 35:

> . . . for the bread of God is that which comes down from heaven, and gives life to the world. . . . I am the bread of life; he who comes to me shall not hunger, and he who believes in me shall never thirst.

It is not mere satisfaction that Jesus offers, a mere sating of the appetite; it is a substance, that 'bread of life' which the world can neither give nor take away. What is important to remember is that Jesus does meet the real need; he feeds the hungry not with metaphors but with food, not with resolutions and presidential commissions but with so much bread and fish that there is an abundance of fish left over. He met the physical needs of his hearers in a generous and open-hearted way so that, their stomachs being full, the hunger of their hearts could be addressed. The message of this miracle is clear: it is not the will of God that people should go hungry. The Gospel is never offered as a substitute for the fundamental needs of human survival, for it is the will of God that those who hunger and thirst should be given food and drink and that they should be provided generously and without stint. The hunger and poverty of this world are not signs of insufficient piety; they are signs that we continue to mismanage the resources that God has given us. The poor rebuke the rich not because the poor are morally superior to the rich, for they are not, but by reminding them that no one is truly rich while anyone is truly poor. Jesus makes it clear that there is a real relationship between the hunger of the body and the hunger of the soul. The spiritual and the physical are each part of the divine concern and the divine plan. Jesus fed the hungry on the mountainside, but while he did not ignore or make light of their physical hunger, he did not stop when that had been satisfied; he went on to meet the hunger of their souls.

What about the hunger of the satisfied? What about the needs of those who 'hunger and thirst after righteousness'? As long as it is possible to define hunger in terms of the absence of loaves and fishes, we can work, pray, and fight to provide enough loaves and fishes for those who need them; but what happens when the satisfied are not satisfied with satisfaction? The miracle of the feeding of the five thousand is that God is willing to provide not only bread but that he is willing to offer the bread of life as well, the food that does not perish but endures to eternal life.

Once again we learn that the fundamental lesson of hospitality is not simply in giving, but in receiving as well that which we most need to have. Jesus offers not simply food to the hungry but himself to us all.

> I am the living bread which came down from heaven; if anyone eats of this bread, he will live forever; and the bread which I shall give for the life of the world is my flesh.

When you are fed at the Holy Communion, remember not only that Jesus fed the hungry on the hillside with loaves and fishes but that by that act of human charity he was revealed to the crowd as God's message of love to the world. To that world he offers not simply sustenance without which our bodies cannot live, but substance without which our souls cannot live. What he offers he gives in himself, and this memorial that we make of his body and blood allows us to become a part of that message, a part of that miracle whereby we, with those who hunger and thirst after righteousness, may yet be filled.

Peter J. Gomes
Sermons – Biblical Wisdom for Daily Living

Proper 15/Ordinary Time 20

Sunday between 14 and 20 August inclusive

John 6:51-58

Christ dwells in me to nourish, guide and enable me, to teach, convince and subdue.

The first 'break-through' came for me at a service held in the 'New Room', Wesley's oldest chapel, in Broadmead, Bristol. The table was spread at 7 am on a weekday in May, so that we might share the sacrament before going to work. A Methodist minister (Leslie Wollen) spoke profoundly and simply of the toil that God had blessed in order to bring the bread to that table. He wonderfully kindled my imagination, and in the silence (for which the rubric provides 'when all have communicated') the sound of the city's traffic, of a ship's siren from the docks, of the hiss of steam from the railway, mingled with the steady tick of the old clock on the gallery, and I saw the wide sweep of the earth which is the Lord's, with all its fullness, making possible and being affected by the eucharistic feast of the people of God.

I cannot count my communions since then. Some stand out in my mind. There was one at a lakeside camp in New Jersey, where the 'church' was a clearing in the forest above the lake, the sanctuary was marked by a fallen oak, the table was a flat rock. The chaplain and I went ahead to prepare the sacrament and, as we waited, the young people began to climb up from below, singing as they came: 'Mine eyes have seen the glory of the coming of the Lord . . .' Maybe they liked the tune and thought of John Brown, whose soul goes marching on. But soon they were quiet for the great invitation: 'Ye that . . . intend to lead a new life, following the commandments of God, and walking from henceforth in his holy ways; draw near with faith . . .' So they drew near, and forgot John Brown's body, and received Christ's to their great and endless comfort.

Another communion was at New Delhi in 1961, when in the Shamiana, a vast tent, three thousand people from all over the world forgot their divisive theories at the adoration of the Lamb, and Indian peasant, British mathematician, American lawyer, German pastor, Nigerian statesman, Korean bishop, knelt together. Another communion was in an English county borough, when, in an upper room, thirty young people met for breakfast, the bread and wine were passed round the table and in the real presence of Christ, the names were read out of those who were going the next day to college, away from home for the first time.

But most communions I cannot remember in particular. I only know that, down the years, they have marked my way. I have been able to think of my life as a journey from one celebration of the sacrament to the next, so that there is no moment when I may not recall the last one and look forward to the one to follow; no experience which does not gain in depth by being seen in the light of the Lord's table. For me, therefore, every road becomes a road to the upper room and every aspect of the Gospel is enriched and expounded more fully at Holy Communion. Every family meal can be enhanced by this meal, every memory purified in this remembrance. Christ's promised presence may be claimed more truly in every place, because his presence is really known here. Life and work derive new significance from the bread broken at this table; the future holds no dread, for Christ has conquered sin and death, and is the Lord in whom all things consist. In fact, whichever way I look, whatever happens, I may in everything give thanks, for the whole universe, at every level, unites in an everlasting Eucharist.

I do not mean to imply that every Holy Communion is, for me, an occasion of unparalleled inspiration and power. There are times when I see my approach to the sacrament as a duty more than a delight. I come to this table with 'weary feet and slow'. Yet how thankful I am for this discipline, this regular setting forth of the objective truths of the Gospel, so that whatever I may *feel*, I can say, 'I have eaten that bread', and Christ dwells in me to nourish, guide and enable me, to teach, convince and subdue.

Dom Gregory Dix, in his great book *The Shape of the Liturgy*, tells how, after the sack of Rome in AD 410, when the world entered the long, dark tunnel of seven barbarian centuries, it was the faith of a Church centred in the Eucharist which shone as a light which no darkness could master. . . .

Where lies the Church amid the world so optimistic and so sad? If humankind avoids global suicide, controls the population, feeds the minds of millions and gives them healthy bodies, where will the Church be in a world whose victories apparently owe nothing to the Church's ministry? If mankind faces the charnel house of a post-nuclear cataclysm, or an earth largely decimated by the opening of a bio-chemical Pandora's box, where will the Church be that seems to have done so little to save the world from the consequences of its sin?

I believe that whether people die defiantly in the darkness of pride or perish miserably in the night of despair; whether they live in the joy of achievement or exist through the midnight of desolation, and yet overcome, the Church will be wherever the Table of the Lord is spread, wherever the eucharistic feast is celebrated. The only true hope is a sacramental hope, for it brings down the mighty from their seat and exalts them of low degree. Humankind 'come of age' is kept humble at this table. Humankind which has no might is increased in strength. The stone that falls to crush all pride, is, for the needy, as the shadow of a great rock in a weary land.

Do not hold back from this table.

Come often. Come now.

Join the pilgrims on the way to the upper room. They're a mixed crowd; no two are the same. But they all have one thing in common. They need the Bread. They must have Christ. They cannot live without him. They dare not die without him.

Can you?

Brian A. Greet
To Communion – with Confidence

Proper 16/Ordinary Time 21

Sunday between 21 and 27 August inclusive

John 6:56-69

The fundamental offence in the work and words of Jesus is the offence of grace.

'He who eats my flesh and drinks my blood has eternal life, and I will raise him up at the last day. For my flesh is food indeed, and my blood is drink indeed. He who eats my flesh and drinks my blood abides in me, and I in him' (John 6:54-56).

What could he mean? Plainly his language was not to be taken literally: he was not advocating cannibalism. But how was it to be taken? It was not only obscure, they thought: it was offensive. For Jews the drinking of any blood, even the eating of flesh from which the blood had not been completely drained, was taboo. But drinking the blood of a human being was an idea that ought not even to be mentioned. This was a hard saying in more senses than one.

Jesus answered their protest by pointing out that his words were to be understood spiritually. 'It is the spirit that gives life, the flesh is of no avail' (John 6:63). The physical or literal meaning of the words was plainly ruled out. But what was the spiritual meaning?

Again, the reader of the Gospel, viewing these words in the context of the whole work, has an advantage over the first hearers, who had no such explanatory context. What we have in Jesus' strange language is a powerful metaphor stating that a share in the life of God, eternal life, is granted to those who in faith come to Jesus, appropriate him, enter into union with him. On this let two doctors of the Church be heard: Augustine of Hippo (at the end of the fourth century) and Bernard of Clairvaux (twelfth century).

The hard saying cannot be taken literally, says Augustine, since it would seem to be enjoining a crime or a vice: 'It is therefore a figure, bidding us to communicate in the sufferings of our Lord, and secretly and profitably treasure in our hearts the fact that his flesh was crucified and pierced for us.' Elsewhere he sums the matter up in an epigram: *Credo et Manducasti*, 'Believe and thou hast eaten'.

Bernard expounds the words, 'He who eats my flesh and drinks my blood has eternal life' as meaning: 'He who reflects on my death, and after my example mortifies his members which are on earth, has eternal life – in other words, "If you suffer with me, you will also reign with me".'

The question is naturally raised: what relation do these

words of Jesus bear to the communion service, in which believers receive bread and wine as tokens of the body and blood of the Lord? Since John, unlike the other evangelists, does not record the institution of the Holy Communion, it could be said that this discourse represents his counterpart to their accounts of what Jesus did and said in the upper room when he gave his disciples the bread and the cup. In the discourse of John 6 Jesus is not making a direct reference to the Holy Communion, but this discourse conveys the same truth in words as the Holy Communion conveys in action. This truth is summed up in the invitation extended to the communicant in the *Book of Common Prayer:* 'Take and eat this in remembrance that Christ died for thee, and feed on him in thy heart by faith with thanksgiving.' To feed on Christ in one's heart by faith with thanksgiving is to 'eat the flesh of the Son of Man and drink his blood' and so have eternal life.

F. F. Bruce
The Hard Sayings of Jesus

Where a messiah was expected, the expectation tended to become defined not by what God would do for the people but by what the people wanted from God. 'When the Messiah comes' is an expression that may unleash a shopping list of the things we desire. So even the category 'messiah' can become corrupted to the point that a confession that Jesus is the Messiah, that he is the one we have been waiting for, is inappropriate to Jesus' own understanding of himself and his mission. To say this is not to comment solely on Jesus' listeners in the synagogue at Capernaum but on ourselves as well.

John 6 elaborates on a theme running through the entire Gospel: the fundamental offence in the work and words of Jesus is the offence of grace. It is sometimes stated gently: we have life from the bread that God gives. It is sometimes stated bluntly, so as to offend all our claims of free will and self-determination: no one can come to me unless that person has been drawn of God (verses 37-40, 44, 65). This is truly the hard saying, but the issue is clear. Do we preside over life, demanding that Jesus do as Moses did, calling for signs as proof so we can decide whether or not to believe, electing Jesus king by our acclamation? Or do we accept the gift from heaven? The bread in the wilderness was a gift; the bread as the Word from heaven was and is a gift; the bread of the Eucharist is a gift. Take, eat and live.

For all who do not walk away, Simon Peter speaks: 'Lord, to whom can we go? You have the words of eternal life. We have come to believe and know that you are the Holy One of God' (verses 68-69).

Fred B. Craddock
Preaching Through the Christian Year: 'B'

Whose table is it?

Pastor Niemoller told the story of how people in the concentration camp asked if he would have a communion service with them. He told how he was puzzled because he was not in communion with all of them. With some, yes, but there were barriers of churchmanship, and he did not want to encourage anyone to break the barriers.

They asked again. Again he thought and prayed over it. He then told them how, while he was praying, it seemed as though a voice from heaven said to him: 'Niemoller, whose table is it? Is it yours or mine?'

He then said, 'I have never since then refused to give communion to any who come'.

Unknown

Proper 17/Ordinary Time 22

Sunday between 28 August and 3 September inclusive

Mark 7:1-8, 14-15, 21-23

No cares or sorrows, no foolish pity or other troubles can touch a heart of stone.

Not long ago the people of the Black Forest still believed in spirits who lived among the trees, and it is only recently that this foolish superstition has been stamped out. Strangely enough, even the spirits who were supposed to live in the Black Forest wore different dress; accordingly, the kindly spirit known as the Little Glass Man, who was just four-and-a-half feet tall, was always said to wear a pointed, wide-brimmed hat, wide breeches, doublet and red stockings, while Dutch Michael, who lived on the other side of the Forest, was thought of as a huge, broad-shouldered fellow, wearing the craftsmen's dress. Several people who claimed to have seen him swore they would not have cared to pay for the calves whose hides must have gone to make Dutch Michael's boots. 'They were so tall, any common man would have been up to his neck in them!' said they, and they swore it was no exaggeration.

My tale concerns a young man from the Black Forest who had dealings with these two spirits, or so the story goes. There was once a widow called Barbara Munk living in the forest. Her husband had been a charcoal burner, and when he died their sixteen-year-old son continued in the same trade. Young Peter Munk had known of no other way of life at home, except to sit with his father over a smoking kiln all week long, or else, covered with soot, go down to town and sell the charcoal, when it was ready. But a charcoal burner has plenty of time for thinking. And Peter Munk thought about himself and he thought about other people as he sat over his kiln. He thought about all the dark trees around him, and the deep silence of the forest moved him to tears and a strange sense of longing. There was something that troubled him – but he hardly knew what. But at last he realised where his trouble lay. It was his humble position in life!

'I'm nothing but a lonely, black-faced charcoal burner!' said he to himself. 'How people look up to the glass blowers and watchmakers, and even the musicians on a Sunday evening! But suppose Peter Munk turned up in the tavern one evening, all washed and clean, in father's best doublet with silver buttons and a pair of new red stockings. And suppose someone came up behind me wondering, "Who's that good looking young man?" And admired my red stockings and the way I walked. Why, no sooner would he get a good look at my face than he'd say, "Oh, it's only Peter the charcaol burner!"'

[Peter becomes very envious of other people. He envies Big Ezekiel his riches; he envies Toll Schlurker his wealth too, but also his daring speeches, for he spoke his mind to anyone and contradicted anyone regardless of their station in life; and he envied the King of the Dance for his dancing ability. How, he often thought, did he suddenly become wealthy? For years he was a poor servant of a timber merchant.

As Peter ponders all of this he remembers the story of the Little Glass Man and goes off in search of him in the forest. When they meet, the Little Glass Man takes pity on Peter and gives him three wishes. But before disappearing says he can only have two for the moment, one has to be held in reserve.

So Peter wishes to dance better than the King of the Dance and always have as much money as Big Ezekiel and to own the finest, richest glass works in the Black Forest. These are all given, but because Peter did not ask for quick wits and good judgement, he soon loses everything.

When the bailiff comes to re-possess all Peter's assets, he runs off to seek help from Dutch Michael, and the following is what transpires.]

'Don't take this amiss!' said Dutch Michael, 'but you've wasted many hundred florins on beggars and such worthless folk, and what good did it do you? They blessed you and wished you good health – and did you feel any better for it? . . . A fine blessing it was when you were sold up and thrown out of your house! And what was it made you put your hand in your pocket whenever a beggarman held out his battered old hat? Your heart, to be sure! Your heart – not your eyes nor your tongue, not your arms nor your legs, but your heart. One might say that you took everything too much to heart!'

'But how can I stop having such feelings?' asked Peter. 'I've tried and tried not to listen to my heart, but it *will* keep beating, and oh! how it hurts!'

'Why, there's nothing you can do, my poor friend!' said Dutch Michael, roaring with laughter. 'But just give me your heart, and you'll find you're much better off.'

'Give you my heart?' cried Peter in horror. 'But then I should die! No, never!'

'Yes, to be sure, you'd die if a surgeon cut the heart out of your body. But I can do better than that. Come this way and see for yourself.'

He stood up, opened a door and led Peter into another

room. Peter's heart nearly failed him as he stepped over the threshold, but he took no notice of it, for a strange sight met his eyes. The room was lined with wooden shelves; on the shelves stood glass jars filled with liquid, and inside each jar was a heart. The jars were all labelled with people's names. Peter read them curiously. There was Big Ezekiel's heart, the head forester's heart, and the King of the Dance's heart, and the bailiff's heart too. He saw six corn chandlers' hearts, eight recruiting sergeants' hearts, three moneylenders' hearts – in short, here was a collection of the most distinguished hearts for fifty miles around.

'Look at these!' said Dutch Michael. 'All these folk have rid themselves of life's cares and sorrows. Not one of these hearts beats in pain or grief any longer.'

'But what do they have in their breasts instead of a heart?' asked Peter, his head fairly reeling with the sights he had seen.

'This!' replied Dutch Michael, and opening a drawer, he showed Peter a heart made of stone.

'What?' cried Peter, unable to repress the shudder that ran down his spine. 'A stone heart? But, Dutch Michael, sir – doesn't it feel very cold?'

'Cold? Well, let's say pleasantly cool! In any case, why should a heart be warm? A warm heart does you no good in winter – a nip of brandy is more use! And you have no notion how refreshing a cold heart can be in the midsummer. Moreover, as I told you, no cares or sorrows, no foolish pity or other troubles can touch a heart of stone.'

[So Peter accepts a bargain: immense wealth in exchange for his heart, replaced by one made of stone. Afterwards he travelled for two years, viewing the sights from left to right of his carriage as he drove by. But nothing could give him any pleasure. Neither fine buildings nor beautiful pictures, nor music nor dancing. His heart of stone took no interest in anything, and his ears and eyes were deadened to all beauty. The only pleasures he had left were in eating and drinking and sleeping. And so he lived, travelling aimlessly through the world, eating just to keep alive and sleeping through sheer boredom.]

Fairy Tales of Wilhelm Hauff

Proper 18/Ordinary Time 23

Sunday between 4 and 10 September inclusive

Mark 7:24-37

*Long familiarity
with this story,
together with the
traditional picture
of the gentleness
of Jesus, tends to
obscure the shock-
ing intolerance of
the saying.*

The saying was a hard one in the first instance to the woman, yet not so hard that it put her off: if Jesus' healing ministry was for Jewish children and not for Gentile dogs, yet she reminded him that the dogs commonly get what the children leave over, and that was what she was asking him to give her and her daughter. To the modern reader it is hard because it seems so inconsistent with the character of Jesus. Its hardness is put in blunt terms by one writer: 'Long familiarity with this story, together with the traditional picture of the gentleness of Jesus, tends to obscure the shocking intolerance of the saying.'

Jesus' Palestinian ministry was directed to the Jewish people. Matthew represents him as saying to the woman, 'I was sent only to the lost sheep of the house of Israel'. There are suggestions here and there in the record of the ministry that, as a sequel to it, blessing would be available to Gentiles too, but very few instances of direct blessing to the Gentiles appear within the context of the ministry itself.

Why did the woman not take offence at such an unpromising reply to her request? One obvious reason was that she was determined to get what she wanted for her daughter. In addition, what if there was a twinkle in his eye as he spoke, as much as to say, 'You know what we Jews are supposed to think of you Gentiles; do you think it is right for you to come and ask for a share in the healing which I have come to impart to Jews?' The written record can preserve the spoken words; it cannot convey the tone of voice in which they were said. Maybe the tone of voice encouraged the woman to persevere.

Again, what are we to say of the term 'dogs'? That is a term of abuse, if ever there was one. The pariah dog was not an estimable animal in Near-Eastern culture then, any more than he is today. But it is not the pariah dogs that are intended here, like those at the door of the rich man in the parable, whose attentions added to Lazarus' afflictions. It is the dogs beneath the table. That in itself might suggest that they are household pets, the children's playmates; and this is confirmed by the fact that the word for 'dogs' used by both Jesus and the woman is diminutive. Since the woman is said by Mark to have been a Greek (i.e. one who spoke Greek), the Greek diminutive used by Mark may have been the word actually used in the conversation.

The woman was quick-witted enough to deduce from Jesus' words the kind of reply to him that would win the granting of her request: 'Sir, even the little dogs under the table eat the leftovers!' The word 'faith' is not mentioned in Mark's account of the incident . . . but the woman's reply expresses just the kind of faith that Jesus so greatly appreciated and that never failed to receive what it asked from him. Jesus was aware of a greater rapport with him on her part than he too often found among his own people. Her daughter was healed immediately, and healed, as in the other instance of Gentile faith in the Synoptic Gospels (that of the Capernaum Centurion and his sick servant), not by direct contact but at a distance.

F. F. Bruce
The Hard Sayings of Jesus

Really there is no point in trying to dodge this issue. Here is a story about unfairness and about injustice.

It is, after all, hardly fair that the young girl should have been invaded and possessed by an unclean spirit. She had no choice in the matter. She was clearly the unfortunate victim of the demonic realm. What kind of justice guides a world like that?

It is, after all, hardly fair that the Syrophoenician woman should have been taken to task for being of Gentile descent. She had no choice in the matter. She was clearly the unfortunate victim of the situation of her birth. What kind of justice guides a world like that?

It is, after all, hardly fair that Jesus should have addressed the woman with such discourtesy and disdain. The age-old history of conflict between Jews and Gentiles was not of her making. She was clearly the unfortunate victim of racism and ethnic stereotyping. What kind of justice guides a world like that?

But then, at last, when God acts decisively in the story, the injustice is reversed. The Syrophoenician woman is treated like one of the children and is no longer left outside like one of the dogs. The young girl is freed from the unclean spirit and is no longer left victim to demonic possession. What kind of God intervenes in a world like that?

This is a story not only about unfairness and injustice, but about God's decisive activity as well.

Leslie J. Francis
Personality Type and Scripture: Exploring Mark's Gospel

Proper 19/Ordinary Time 24

Sunday between 11 and 17 September inclusive

Mark 8:27-38

It is never enough to know what other people have said about Jesus. . . . To every one Jesus comes asking, not, 'Can you tell me what others have said and written about me?' but, 'Who do you say that I am?'

This is one of the most crucial moments in the life of Jesus. He asked this question when he was already turning his face to go to Jerusalem. He well knew what awaited him there, and the answer to his question was of supreme importance. He *knew* that he was going to a cross to die; he *wanted to know* before he went, if there was anyone who had really discovered who he was. The right answer would make all the difference. If instead there was dull incomprehension, all his work would have gone for nothing. If there was any realisation, however incomplete, it meant that he had lit such a torch in the hearts of men and women as time would never put out. How Jesus' heart must have lifted when Peter's sudden discovery rushed to his lips – 'You are the anointed one of God!' When Jesus heard that, he knew he had not failed.

Not only had the Twelve to discover the fact; they had also to discover what the fact meant. They had grown up against a background of thought which expected from God a conquering king who would lead them to world dominion. Peter's eyes would blaze with excitement when he said this. But Jesus had to teach them that God's anointed one had come to die upon a cross. He had to take their ideas of God and of God's purposes and turn them upside down; and from this time that is what he set himself to do. They had discovered who he was; now they had to learn what that discovery meant.

There are two great general truths in this passage.

(i) Jesus began by asking what men were saying about him; and then, suddenly, he flashes the question at the Twelve, 'Who do *you* say that I am?' It is never enough to know what other people have said about Jesus. A person might be able to pass any examination on what has been said and thought about Jesus; they might have read every book about Christology written in every language upon earth and still not be a Christian. Jesus must always be our own personal discovery. Our religion can never be a carried tale. To every one Jesus comes asking, not, 'Can you tell me what others have said and written about me?' but, 'Who do *you* say that I am?' Paul did not say, 'I know *what* I have believed', he said, 'I know *whom* I have believed' (2 Timothy 1:12). Christianity does not mean reciting a creed; it means knowing a person.

(ii) Jesus said, 'I must go to Jerusalem and die'. It is of the greatest interest to look at the times in Luke's Gospel when Jesus said *must*. 'I *must* be in my Father's house' (2:49). 'I *must* preach the kingdom' (4:43). 'I *must* go on my way today and tomorrow' (13:33). Over and over again he told his disciples he *must* go to his cross (9:22; 17:25; 24:7). Jesus knew he had a destiny to fulfil. God's will was his will. He had no other object but to do upon earth what God had sent him to do. Christians, like their Lord, are people under orders.

William Barclay
Luke: Daily Study Bible

This passage can only be understood if full weight is given to its position at the opening of a new section of the Gospel. In the first section we have heard of a whole series of deeds and incidents in the life of Jesus which raise the question: Who then *is* this that he can do such things? (cf. Mark 4:41 for example). Indeed, according to St Mark, the career of Jesus had raised the question so inescapably that even *men* (verse 27) – i.e. ordinary people, people who made no pretence of being disciples – had found themselves not only asking it, but forced to answer that Jesus must be some very great figure indeed, John the Baptist or one of the great prophets risen from the dead (verse 28). But even such guesses did not go far enough; for even the Baptist and the prophets did no more than pave the way for the one who would actually *bring* the salvation to which they pointed forward. And those who were admitted to the full truth about Jesus realised that his was the final role of fulfilment, of the *achievement* of salvation. The true, and specifically Christian, answer to the question posed by Jesus is: '*You are* (nothing less than) *the Messiah*' (verse 29).

Since these words express the Christian understanding of Jesus, we might have expected that they would be met with an enthusiastic and unambiguous acknowledgement from Jesus himself, and in St Matthew's version of the story that is exactly what happens (Matthew 16:17); the opening of the second section of the Gospel would then provide a simple and authoritative answer to the question posed by the first section. In St Mark's version, however, the incident is much more complex: Jesus' immediate reaction to the disciples' confession is ambiguous; he swears them to silence about himself (verse 30). On the one hand this implies a tacit acceptance of their description of him, but on the other hand, it will be noticed that he studiously avoids taking the title *Messiah* on his own lips; and in the Greek, the word used for *charging* the disciples to tell no one normally means 'rebuke', suggesting a hint of censure and displeasure; there was apparently some sense in which he was not, and did not wish to be known as, Messiah. The sequel helps to make clear what that sense was. However exactly the term *Messiah* was understood at the time – and, as we have seen, different groups understood it in different ways – there was general agreement that the Messiah would accomplish his work by the possession and exercise of brute power in one form or another – power is none the less power for being directly supplied from heaven – he would be a glorious and manifestly victorious figure to whom defeat and suffering would be entirely foreign. The disciples' confession therefore presents Jesus with a dilemma. In so far as it is a matter of choosing between Peter's description of him and the lesser descriptions of *men*, he must accept the higher title, for he *is* the final Saviour, to whom all previous religious leaders pointed forward. Yet in its normal sense he cannot accept the title; and since it is at least partly in that sense that his disciples apply the title to him, he must 'rebuke' them and forbid them to make their confession public. For his part he apparently prefers the title *Son of man* which probably at the time smacked less of military and political methods and purely worldly success. In any case, whatever title is to be used, he hastens to remove any false impressions by proclaiming unambiguously that his earthly future would be one of ignominy, defeat, and suffering (verses 31-32a).

It is now the turn of the disciples to react with shocked and strongly felt disapproval. Acting once again through their spokesman Peter, they in their turn *rebuke* Jesus for such ideas (verse 32 – same Greek word as in verse 30) and attempt to dissuade him from them. If he really is Messiah, they imply, any thought of such a future must be wrong. The blistering severity of Jesus' reply is evidence enough that what is at stake is a matter of quite central importance, and that in two ways.

In the first place, when Jesus said *must* in verse 31 he meant what he said. He used the word in a sense in which it was often used in contemporary apocalyptic literature, as showing that certain future events were part of the firmly decreed will of God. Thus, to persuade Jesus to shrink from those events was to tempt him to disobey the will of God, as Satan had done in the wilderness.

Secondly, we have to ask *why* the disciples were so vehemently opposed to the suggestion that Jesus must suffer. The very vehemence of their opposition is meant to suggest that it is more than a matter of the intellect, more than a simple failure to understand what Jesus meant; the disciples did not *want* Jesus to suffer. And that was because it goes against the grain to be the followers of a Messiah who suffers instead of producing spectacular victories by an effortless exercise of power; it brings no kudos, and offends the pride of the natural human. And judged by ordinary standards, there seems no point in the suffering and death of the Messiah. What is more, if it is the will of God that the Messiah should suffer, it might well be his will that the Messiah's disciples should suffer a similar fate; from that again the natural human shrinks. So by their reaction to Jesus' prophecy the disciples reveal even more clearly than before the truth about themselves, that their minds and wills are governed by the standards of this world, of the unredeemed, natural human – 'they think as men think' (verse 33).

What they have got to be taught, therefore, is that 'God thinks otherwise' – that his standards of judgement and ways of going about things are completely the reverse of those accepted in the world. And since this is something all need to know, and there is no secrecy about it, the crowd is called in to share the lesson (verse 34a). In the following verses (8:34b-9:1) this is enlarged on. The only way to attain 'life' – i.e. true life, the life of the age to come – is through trust in God and obedience to his will. But since that must involve suffering and death in this world, the only way to get life is by behaving in a way which seems to unredeemed humankind unintelligent and self-defeating: willingly accepting loss and injury in the cause of Christ and his Gospel, and refusing to bend all one's energies, as other people do, to preserving, securing, and enriching one's life in this world. No one can pretend that this is easy; we are all afraid of pain and suffering, and 'ashamed' of seeming fools to our fellows. But let the Christian remember what is at stake – even the life of this world is worth more than everything else in existence – how much more the life of the age to come? (verses 36-37). And let the disciple remember that this is the only way; this age is thoroughly contrary to the will of God (verse 38) and if anyone is ashamed of Christ in deference to its standards they can expect only one verdict when the day of reckoning comes (verse 38). And come it will very soon; and with it the establishment of God's kingdom with power and the end of suffering for the Christian; those who persevere will not have long to wait (9:1).

There can be no doubt that this section was constructed by St Mark out of separate items or tradition and that in constructing it his purpose was to bring out two, or rather perhaps three, important truths.

(a) That although the answer to the question posed in the first section of the Gospel may be, indeed *must* be, put in the form: 'Jesus is the Messiah', that is only the true answer if the title Messiah is understood in the sense of Jesus' favourite self-designation *Son of man* as implying the necessity of redemptive suffering and death.

(b) That the disciples' failure to understand Jesus' teaching on the subject of suffering is only another manifestation of the hardening of their hearts and of their domination by the power of Satan and the values of this world.

(c) The story is not so much intended to describe faithfully what happened on the *first* occasion when Jesus was recognised as Messiah as to show what is essentially involved and demanded whenever such a recognition takes place. In that connection it is particularly important to keep in mind the immediately preceding story of the opening of the blind man's eyes. Just as then it was Jesus who gradually enabled the blind man to see, so here it is Jesus who by his repeated question and his teaching gradually reveals to the disciples the fact, nature, and implications of his Messiahship. To see Jesus for what he really is, and to know how to respond, is always a gift of God in Christ.

D. E. Nineham:
St Mark: The Pelican Gospel Commentaries

Proper 20/Ordinary Time 25

Sunday between 18 and 24 September inclusive

Mark 9:30-37

He looked around at [them] now and the sad gentleness of his face affected them deeply.

Monday, 4 October 1813

In the centre of the Indian encampment, off to one side of Proctor's army, Tecumseh sat before the fire, not joining in the conversation but merely smoking his pipe. Close by sat Wasegoboah, husband of his sister Tecumapese, and beside him was Chau-be-nee, his most trusted lieutenant. Although there was some excitement in the eyes and talk of many of the younger men over the impending battle, none of this was reflected in the forty-five-year old Tecumseh.

One of the younger Indians, known by the name of Billy Caldwell, spoke eagerly to Tecumseh. 'Father, what are we to do? Shall we fight the Americans?'

Tecumseh nodded slowly. 'Yes, my son, on the morrow we will be in their smoke.'

He was silent for a handful of minutes more, and then, as if reaching a decision he had been long considering, he stood. At once the assemblage came to a respectful silence.

'My children,' he said, 'hear me well. Tomorrow we go into our final battle with the Americans. In this battle I will be killed.'

There was an instant murmur of consternation among them, but Tecumseh silenced it and went on: 'You are my friends, my people. I love you too well to see you sacrificed in an unequal contest from which no good can result. I would dissuade you from fighting this fight, encourage you to leave now, this night, for there is no victory ahead, only sorrow. Yet, time after time, even until tonight, you have made known to me that it is your desire to fight the Americans here and so I am willing to go with my people and be guided by their wishes.'

He then began to remove every sign of rank which he wore: medals, bracelets, necklaces, insignia, the two-feathered headband. They watched him in silence as each item was removed until, finally, he stood before them in his simple tanned buckskin leggings, frock shirt and moccasins. His knife he gave to Chief Roundhead. His tomahawk went to Black Hawk.

His sword he handed to Chau-be-nee and said, 'When my

son Pugeshashenwa becomes a noted warrior and able to wield a sword, give this to him.'

He looked around at the others now and the sad gentleness of his face affected them deeply, for all wore mournful expressions and the eyes of many were bright with tears still unshed. All he had retained of his possessions was his favourite weapon, the war club he had carried since the early days of fighting beside his brother Chiksika. He told them that he was now divested of all rank and ornamentation which might identify him as Tecumseh. Then he took the ramrod from his rifle lying nearby and handed it to Wasegoboah.

'When you see me fall,' he instructed, 'fight your way to my side and strike my body four times with this rod. If you will do so, I will then arise and, with my life renewed and charmed against further harm, will lead you to victory. But should I fall and this cannot be done, then retreat at once, for further fighting will be useless.'

With a sense of awe, Wasegoboah accepted the ramrod and promised that he would stay close to his chief and that when Tecumseh should fall, he would come to his side at once and strike the four blows as directed.

Not one of the Indians present had any doubt that if Tecumseh did fall and his body was struck with the rod, he would arise as he had indicated. They had long ago learned to accept the mysterious predictions from their chief without question. After all, had they not always come true?

Allan W. Eckert
The Frontiersmen

Tecumseh was the last great Shawnee chief who tried to unify the Indian tribes for one last stand against the Americans. He did predict his own death, the place and the manner of it. Everything happened as he had foretold.

Jesus took a little child in his arms and said to the disciples, 'Whoever welcomes one such child in my name welcomes me.' So where do you see that welcome today?

Do you see that welcome in schools, as dedicated teachers care for and shape young lives? Is Jesus truly welcomed there?

Do you see that welcome in children's hospital wards, as specialist nurses and doctors care for and heal young lives? Is Jesus truly welcomed there?

Do you see that welcome in the leaders of voluntary groups, like the Cubs and the Brownies, as the Brown Owl and Akela care for and shape young lives? Is Jesus truly welcomed there?

Do you see that welcome in counsellors and social workers, as they try to deal with the trauma and distress of young lives? Is Jesus truly welcomed there?

Do you see the welcome in the international care agencies, as child poverty, child abuse and child exploitation are brought on to the political agenda? Is Jesus truly welcomed there?

Do you see that welcome in the local church, as infants, children and adolescents are fully embraced as rightful members of the family of God? Is Jesus truly welcomed there?

Jesus took a young child in his arms and said to the disciples, 'Whoever welcomes one such child in my name welcomes me.' So where do you see that welcome today?

Leslie J. Francis
Personality Type and Scripture: Exploring Mark's Gospel

Proper 21/Ordinary Time 26

Sunday between 23 September and 1 October inclusive

Mark 9:38-50

John has always had his successors in the Church, who feel unhappy when things are done in Jesus' name by people whose authority to do them they cannot recognise.

For or against

There is no formal contradiction between 'He who is not with me is against me' and 'He that is not against us is for us' (or, as Luke has it, 'He that is not against you is for you'). In a situation where no neutrality is possible, people must be either on one side or on the other, so that those who are not for are against, and those who are not against are for. But there is a difference in emphasis between the two ways of expressing this.

The former saying comes in a context where Jesus is speaking of the conflict between the Kingdom of God and the forces of evil. This is a conflict in which no one should be neutral. Since Jesus is the divinely appointed agent for leading the battle against the forces of evil, those who wish to see the triumph of God's cause must follow him. If they do not, then whatever they may think themselves, they are effectively on the enemy's side. As for the added words about gathering and scattering, gathering is the work of God, while scattering is the work of Satan. God is the God of peace; Satan is the author of strife. 'The Kingdom of God is the one constructive unifying redemptive power in a distracted world; and everyone has to choose whether they will take sides with it or against it.' (T. W. Manson *The Sayings of Jesus*, p. 87, second edition, 1949.)

The latter saying ('He that is not against us is for us') is related to the same subject, although it comes in the course of a narrative, as the punch line in what is sometimes called a 'pronouncement story'. The story is told, that is to say, for the sake of the pronouncement to which it leads up. Here, then, we have such a punch line. John, one of the two 'sons of thunder' . . . tells Jesus that he and his companions saw someone casting out demons in Jesus' name, 'and we forbade him, because he was not following us' (Mark 9:38). In other words, he was not one of the regularly recognised disciples of Jesus. But he was showing clearly which side he was on in the spiritual warfare; moreover, he was acknowledging the authority of Jesus, because it was in his name that he was casting out demons. This was a far cry from the spirit that ascribed Jesus' demon-expelling power to the aid of Beelzebub.

By his words and actions he was showing himself to be on Jesus' side . . . John has always had his successors in the Church, who feel unhappy when things are done in Jesus' name by people whose authority to do them they cannot recognise. But Jesus' reply remains sufficient to silence this attitude: 'No one who does a mighty work in my name will be able soon after to speak evil of me' (Mark 9:39).

F. F. Bruce
The Hard Sayings of Jesus

Saltless salt

One can use salt to season meat or bread, but if the salt one might use for this purpose loses its saltness, what can be used to season it?

But how can salt lose its saltness? If it is truly salt, of course, it must remain salt and retain its saltness. But probably in the ordinary experience of Galilean life, salt was rarely found in a pure state; in practice it was mixed with other substances, various forms of earth. So long as the proportion of salt in the mixture was sufficiently high, the mixture would serve the purpose of true salt. But if, through exposure to damp or some other reason, all the salt in the mixture was leached out, what was left was good for nothing. As Luke, in his amplified version of the saying, puts it, 'it is fit neither for the land nor for the dunghill' (Luke 14:35). It might have been though that the dunghill was all that it was fit for, but Jesus may have used a word that meant 'manure': 'it is no good for the land, not even as manure.'

. . . The figure of insipid salt appears in the words of the rabbis, with reference (it seems) to Israel's role as the salt or purifying agency among the nations of humankind. Matthew's version of Jesus' saying begins with the words: 'You are the salt of the earth' (Matthew 5:13) addressed to his disciples. This implies that the disciples have a particular function to perform on earth, and that, if they fail to perform it, they might as well not exist, for all the good they will do. In what respect they are to be salt is not specified, so the nature of their function has to be inferred from the context and from what is known of the effect of salt. They may be intended to have a preserving and purifying effect on their fellows, or to add zest to the life of the community, or to be a force for peace. The idea of an insipid Christian ought to be a contradiction in terms. One way in which the quality of saltness can be manifested is in one's language. 'Let your speech be always gracious, seasoned with salt', Paul writes to the Colossians (Colossians 4:6) where the salt seems to be that ready Christian wit or wisdom (specially apt in the answering of questions about the faith), which is far removed from the slanderous and unsavoury talk deprecated earlier in the same letter (Colossians 3:8).

. . . Then, after the saying about the salt that has lost its saltness, Mark concludes this series of sayings with 'Have salt in yourselves, and be at peace with one another'. Again, we should understand this injunction better if we knew the situation in which it was originally spoken. 'Have salt in yourselves' might mean 'have salt among yourselves' and might refer to the eating of salt together which was an expression of fellowship at table and therefore of peaceful relations. If this is so, then 'be at peace with one another' is a non-figurative explanation of 'have salt among yourselves'. But we cannot be sure.

F. F. Bruce
The Hard Sayings of Jesus

Proper 22/Ordinary Time 27

Sunday between 2 and 8 October inclusive

Mark 10:2-16

Behind those words 'honour everyone' lies the belief that, if God is our creator, nothing we can do can entirely deface his image in us.

Man lives in the herd. He is one of the crowd, and the supreme torture is isolation from his kind. But in his inmost self he desires something more, something deeper than the casual association with the many, and the close friendship of the few. He wants one friend with whom he stands unchallengeably first, one friend upon whom he can utterly depend, who will love him to the end, whatever he becomes, whether he sinks to obscurity or rises to the height of success: someone who will love him with utter loyalty and stand at his side, even if he is disgraced, shamed and forsaken by the whole world . . . *he wants his wife.*

Similarly, with the woman. *She wants her husband*: no shining knight of heroic splendour and gallant form, but one upon whose loyalty to her she cannot merely rely, but which is of such a kind that it will never cross her mind to question its reliability. He may be a very unromantic figure, whom age has robbed of all physical attraction, whose habits and mannerisms are commonplace and even exasperating. But she wants to know that there is someone in the world's wilderness whose unfaltering friendship she can take as an assured fact . . . a love that will never forsake her.

Bishop of Chelmsford
Quoted by Rita F. Snowden in *People are people*

At a late nineteenth century wedding (around 1887) at Restharrow, Oxfordshire, the bride and groom (Arnold and Bess) along with relatives and friends, walked across the fields to the church.

As they approached the church, the clerk said to Arnold the bridegroom: 'Here 'em come, an I see 'em bringing two vartues along wi' 'em, Charity and Mercy (two relatives as bridesmaids). 'Pity you ain't got no Patience, that'd be the one to stand by 'ee in Holy Matrimony.'

Flora Thompson
Still Glides the Stream

You must thank – or blame – Master Gibbens (His Honour Judge Brian Gibbens 1912-1985) for my sermon this morning. It was after service last Sunday that he said he found it difficult to 'take' the phrase that comes in the blessing I always use at the end of the service: 'Go forth into the world in peace; be of good courage; hold fast that which is good; render to no one evil for evil; strengthen the fainthearted; support the weak . . . Honour everyone'; and he cited certain people he has had up before him of late, and has had to sentence, and asked, understandably, 'Do you really expect me to honour such as these?' It was a worthwhile question.

To begin to formulate some sort of an answer I would like to indulge in a kind of guessing game. I want to tell you about someone, but I leave you to guess who I'm talking about!

His mother lavished love upon him. His father was a customs officer, strict, exacting and unapproachable, who often whipped his son. As a child, the boy particularly loved to play 'Cowboys and Indians'. He was brought up as a devout Catholic, and delighted in the splendour and solemnity of the church festivals. For a time he wanted to be a priest. He was taken to his first opera when he was a boy of 12, and it wasn't long before he knew the whole of Wagner's *The Ring* almost by heart. He was an above-average pianist, and wrote several plays and the libretto of an opera. Bernard Shaw's *St Joan* was one of his favourite plays. When he left school he often went to concerts with his great friend, whose boys he offered to educate when later in life he – my subject – made his name. His father died when he was 13. His mother died of cancer when he was 18. In the last weeks of her life her son did most of the nursing, and drew a picture of her on her deathbed. He said to the doctor who attended her that he would be grateful to him for the rest of his life, and he kept his word, according him special favours when he was in a position to do so. He wanted to become a student in the great Academy of Art in the main city of his land, but a year's preparatory study on his own ended with the rejection of his application. He often went hungry. For a couple of years he was virtually destitute, living in doss houses, and making what money he could by selling postcard views of the city scenes he had sketched and painted. By good fortune, in 1910 an aunt withdrew her savings from the bank, and gave her 21-year-old nephew a good deal of it. He got good lodgings and began to work solidly in watercolours and oils, and sold everything he completed to dealers. Poverty and need had turned the young artist into rather a radical in political terms; but with the outbreak of the war there wasn't time for art or politics. He joined up, and was soon thrown into the battle of Ypres. His courage knew no bounds, and he won high military decorations for bravery. He was gassed and temporarily blinded. When the war ended, he was 30.

With the end of the Great War, and unemployed, he took up politics again. A spell in prison was as creative for him as it was for John Bunyan, and he occupied himself with reading and writing. Out of prison, recognition quickly came to him. On his fiftieth birthday the Pope sent him congratulations; and the cardinal ordered a Te Deum to be sung in the local cathedral when he narrowly escaped death at the hands of a would-be assassin. He was able to say to the end: 'I am a Catholic, and will always remain so.'

Four women attempted suicide for love of him – three successfully; but he didn't in fact marry until shortly before his death. He was always particularly good with the children of his immediate circle of friends; and, just before he died he had some of his friends' children with him.

I expect you've guessed who I've had in mind: Adolf Hitler.

And I've given you this very selective biography of him, because I have never known anyone myself, no matter how lawless, no matter how sinful, who hasn't had what we call 'redeeming features'. And *pantas timesate* – 'honour everyone' – does not mean ignore what is evil about people; it lays down the obligation of the respect and courtesy due to human personality as such; an obligation which is inconsistent, in the political sphere, with those principles of absolute or totalitarian government, such as National Socialism, which sacrifice the individual wholly to the state; and inconsistent, in the economic sphere, with all systems and methods which regard people as 'hands', mere cogs in a machine.

Behind those words 'honour everyone' lies the belief that, if God is our creator, nothing we can do can entirely deface his image in us. Nothing can entirely remove that in us which is worthy of honour; or, indeed, that which may one day be restored to what it was always intended to be.

Eric James
Judge not: A Selection of Sermons

Proper 23/Ordinary Time 28

Sunday between 9 and 15 October inclusive

Mark 10:17-31

Surely Jesus must be joking: who would benefit from behaviour like that?

Live dangerously for a few moments and imagine what it would be like to exchange your worldly possessions for treasure in heaven.

Live dangerously and give away your job to help the unemployed. Free yourself from the drudgery of the workplace to serve full-time in the kingdom of God. But surely Jesus must be joking: who would benefit from behaviour like that?

Live dangerously and give away your car to help the immobile. Free yourself from polluting the atmosphere and burning up the world's oil resources. But surely Jesus must be joking: who would benefit from behaviour like that?

Live dangerously and give away your wardrobe to clothe the naked. Free yourself from the vanity of deciding what to wear each day. But surely Jesus must be joking: who would benefit from behaviour like that?

Live dangerously and give away the contents of your freezer and of your larder to feed the hungry. Free yourself from the anxiety of deciding what to eat each day. But surely Jesus must be joking: who would benefit from behaviour like that?

Live dangerously and give away your home to house the homeless. Free yourself from the stranglehold of mortgage repayments, water rates, council taxes and home insurance policies.

But surely Jesus must be joking: who would benefit from behaviour like that?

Live dangerously for a few moments and imagine what it would be like to exchange your worldly possessions for treasure in heaven.

Leslie J. Francis
Personality Type and Scripture: Exploring Mark's Gospel

192

On our own, what can we do to give the voiceless their say, and to promote a society without castes? With the whole people of God, collectively, it is possible to light a fire on the earth. One of Christ's questions hits home. When the poor person was hungry, did you recognise him? Where were you when I was sharing the life of the utterly destitute? Have you been the oppressor of even one single human being? When I said 'Woe to the rich' – rich in money, or rich in dogmatic certainties – did you prefer the illusions of wealth?

Your struggle cannot be lived out in the ideas that fly from pillar to post and never become reality.

Free from oppression the poor and the exploited, and to your astonishment you will see signs of resurrection springing up, here and now.

Share all you have for greater justice.

Roger Schutz (Brother Roger of Taizé)
Parable of Community

Gluttony at first sight looks like a survival from our animal ancestry. Certainly the urgent drive to search for food is one of the most powerful of animal instincts. But in fact excessive eating such as is common to humans is rarely if ever found among animals, except those domesticated by people and so influenced by them. Men and women commonly overeat, at least in countries where there is an abundance of food, to fill the void caused by loneliness or boredom. This is even truer of excessive drinking. 'The gin shop is the quickest way out of Manchester.' Eating and drinking, despite excess, are clearly good and necessary. This is seen conspicuously when food and drink are shared in a meal between friends or in a family. It is not without reason that heaven has been likened to a feast.

Covetousness is an undue desire to possess. It gives to money or possessions, which are essentially only means to living, the value of ends, of objects to be clung to for their own sake. It can be powered by more than one motive. Avarice, like pride, can be an attempt to escape from the painful sense of insignificance and of dependence on the whim of others. The power which money gives and the wealth which surrounds the rich can help a person to maintain the image of their superiority. But like lust, the urge to possess may have as its underlying motive the desire to escape from loneliness, from the fear of being unloved or even of being unlovable. Money, it is felt, can buy friendship, though in fact it is singularly unsuccessful in doing this. For the rich, though they can buy the company of their fellows, become painfully aware that their so-called friends love their money and the comfort it can obtain more than themselves. Wealth, especially when sought diligently and acquired with effort, tends to separate those who have it from those who have not. It makes the poor envious and the rich defensive. Covetousness has been called idolatry, for it has a unique power of blinding people to their dependence on God and their need to love and be loved by their fellows. The splash of wealth can distract the rich from the needs of the poor and make them forget their humanity. Wealth also appears to be a source of perpetual anxiety. Our Western world has been called an acquisitive society because its economic system, for its efficient working, seems to require the constant stimulation, by means of advertising for example, of the desire to possess more and more. Nevertheless, despite all that can be said against either human avarice or the capital system, both possessions and money are means to the enhancement of human life. Seen as servants of human welfare they are to be valued. But recognised as powerful servants, ever liable to usurp the position of master, they need to be kept firmly in their subordinate place. We live at a time when science and technology have together enabled people to create immense wealth. It may be that the future of human life on this planet depends on the wisdom and determination really to subordinate the new-found wealth to the well-being of the race.

Christopher Bryant SSJE
The Heart in Pilgrimage

Proper 24/Ordinary Time 29

Sunday between 16 and 22 October inclusive

Mark 10:35-45

Past teaching and impending fate are joined in one statement about Jesus' entire purpose: to serve, to die, to set free.

Between last Sunday's Gospel and the reading before us is Mark's account of the third and last prediction of the passion (Mark 10:32-34). With that prediction and the story of James and John, this entire section of Mark (Mark 8:27-10:45) comes to a close. Following Jesus' first prediction (Mark 8:31), Simon Peter strongly objects and rebukes Jesus. Following the second (Mark 9:31), the Twelve engage in a discussion as to who is the greatest. And now after the third and most detailed of the predictions, James and John ask for the favoured positions in glory. With their request, the blindness, not only of the Twelve but of the inner circle (Peter, James, John) in particular, is complete. Also complete is the vast difference between Jesus and his followers on the nature of the messianic mission. In the crisis, they will abandon him (Mark 14:50). Some scholars believe Mark has taken a position over the Twelve and the Church they represent. More likely, Mark is addressing a Church that, though having the advantage of hindsight, has not embraced the cross as the definition not only of the Messiah but of discipleship as well . . .

In response to the request of James and John, Jesus promises suffering but cannot guarantee positions in glory. To describe that suffering, Jesus uses two Old Testament metaphors: the cup of wrath (Isaiah 51:17; Lamentations 4:21) and baptism in the overwhelming flood (Psalm 42:7; 69:1-2; Isaiah 43:2). Here Jesus may be drawing on current views on the messianic woes that would initiate the eschatological age.
. . . Verse 45 closes not only this lection but also this entire section of Mark. It is appropriate to the immediate context in that it presents Jesus as the Son of Man whose entire mission is to serve, not to be served. However, this verse transcends the context in that Jesus' giving of himself has salvific value, unlike the serving and dying of his disciples. The death of Jesus, says Mark, is a ransom; that is, his death sets free captives and hostages. The statement launches, but does not contain within itself, elaborate theories of atonement. Almost as significant as the content of verse 45 is its location in the Gospel. Predictions of the passion are past; instructions about discipleship are past. With Jerusalem and Golgotha now

within view, past teaching and impending fate are joined in one statement about Jesus' entire purpose: to serve, to die, to set free.

Fred B. Craddock
Preaching Through the Christian Year: 'B'

Edward Scissorhands: Christology from a Suburban Fairy Tale

A brief plot outline will highlight the Jesus parallels. A master inventor, played by Vincent Price, creates from various parts, both human and mechanical, what is intended to be a good young man. . . . The inventor is old and has had to work long and hard to perfect the young man's hands. In the meantime, Edward has been using large scissor shears. As he is about to fit the hands, the inventor has a heart attack, collapses and dies, Edward piercing one of the hands that are never to be his. Edward grieves that he does not have hands . . .

The inventor, however, had educated Edward well, infusing his mind with both the wonders of poetic and scientific nature. 'Up there,' in a castle on a hill, Edward lives alone until a sweet Avon lady, Dianne Wiest, invites him down into the world – a pastel 'little boxes' American suburb – to live with her family. Edward, with his pasty complexion, his unruly black hair and his eccentric matching black clothes, appears too different from ordinary people. But he soon wins them over, especially with his tonsorial skills, wielding his scissors on shaggy dogs who then look like show champions, on shrubs and on bored housewives' hairdos. His designs for humans, animals and plants alike are masterpieces.

The daughter of the house, Kim (Winona Ryder) befriends him and becomes lovingly devoted. Her macho boyfriend, Jim (Anthony Michael Hall) is jealous and traps Edward into participating in a robbery. Edward's days down in the suburbs are numbered.

Edward has tried to be human amongst humans, bringing the best out of most of the people he encounters. But then they turn against him. Edward is saved by Kim but has to defend his life against the angry Jim who falls to his death. Kim leaves Edward alone, back in his castle heights. She sends the hostile crowd away telling them that Edward is dead.

However, it is she, as an old woman, who is recounting the story to her granddaughter, keeping alive his memory and his spirit. Edward continues to shape beautiful gardens and ice sculptures. Kim dances in her memories in falling snow.

Here is part of the interpretation of Edward Scissorhands: Jim, Kim's boyfriend, is the betrayer, even persuading Kim for some time to be part of his scheme. He is violent and rude and plans a robbery, inducing the good-natured Edward to be part of it, allowing him to be trapped by security guards with the aim of having him arrested. He would be rid of him. Jim offers Edward his mock kiss.

The fickle women turn against him. Their leader, Joyce, regards him lustfully – an episode which echoes the story of Potiphar's wife and her denunciation of the patriarch, Joseph, who refused to succumb to her seduction (Genesis 39:7-20). This story of the innocent betrayed seems to be archetypal as well. Joyce's malice spurs the women on. Esmerelda, the strange religious fanatic whom people ignored, is now listened to as she denounces Edward. Jim baits him. Edward's shears, which have been such an instrument of joy in shaping and designing, now accidentally strike Kevin and the crowd scents blood. Edward is pursued to his castle as the crowd, now a mob, want his blood. One might say he is pursued like a lamb to the slaughter. *He was their servant*, but he is now suffering – bearing the projection of all their inadequacy and hostility (Isaiah 53:6). It is not hard to hear the echoes of 'Crucify him'. The screenplay makes its parallels with Jesus' passion quite clear.

Clive Marsh and Gaye Ortiz
Exploration in Theology and films

Proper 25/Ordinary Time 30

Sunday between 23 and 29 October inclusive

Mark 10:46-52

Bartimaeus was an outsider who stands in sharp and favourable contrast to the insiders in Mark.

The healing of Bartimaeus is especially significant for those who sit outside the church. Because interpreters deal most often with persons who are at least nominal disciples they may tend to overlook the fact that Bartimaeus was an outsider who stands in sharp and favourable contrast to the insiders in Mark. The text calls attention to persons who, though lost in the crowd, may be ready and eager for some vital contact with Jesus Christ. It is significant that, while many rebuked Bartimaeus' cries and tried to silence him, Jesus, though going steadfastly up to Jerusalem (Mark 10:32) took time to call him.

For either outsiders or insiders, 'What do you want me to do for you?' underlines the importance of getting our deepest desires straight. James and John (Mark 10:35-37) did not; but Bartimaeus did (Mark 10:51f). His responses, first to Jesus' question and then to his command, show that he wanted the right thing; and he wanted it the right way. He did not secretly cherish his infirmity. He really wanted to be healed. 'Prayer is the soul's sincere desire, uttered or unexpressed.' Bartimaeus expressed his prayer persistently, plainly and honestly, 'and immediately he received his sight. . . .' The healing of the blind Bartimaeus is not simply a vivid story with a moral for Christians; it is a witness for Jesus Christ and a call to follow him.

One must not push too far the idea that through his recognition of Jesus as master Bartimaeus acquired spiritual vision and became an ideal disciple. At the cross, he, with all the other disciples, will flee. Yet at this point in the story Bartimaeus' perception as an outsider stands in vivid contrast to the blindness of the disciples as insiders. Furthermore, 'he received his sight' stands in close, parallel relationship to 'followed him on the way'. The text is an invitation to come to Jesus and to see; to see and so to follow Jesus.

Lamar Williamson, Jun.
Mark: Interpretation Bible Commentary

For nine exciting, sometimes difficult, sometimes dangerous years (during major riots) I was a Methodist prison chaplain. During that time I served in HM prisons in Devon and South Yorkshire, meeting a wide variety of inmates from petty thieves to murderers, from con-men to drug addicts.

Apart from my statutory duties of visiting inmates in the prison hospital and segregation unit and interviewing them on arrival, I also ran a Friday night discussion group. About a dozen inmates would meet with me and we would work carefully through each of the Gospels; and doing this with men who quite often had never ever read one or heard one proved a most stimulating and interesting experience. In the course of nine years we all liked Matthew best and on many occasions we discussed his telling of the healing of blind Bartimaeus.

The one question of Jesus to Bartimaeus that I regularly focused the men's attention on was, 'What do you want me to do for you?'

I would remind the men that where two or three met in the name of Jesus, he promised to be there as well. 'So,' I would say, 'he is here with us and he looks into your eyes and asks *you* personally, "What do you want me to do for you?" How will you respond? What will you ask of him?'

Quite often there would be a stunned silence. One inmate actually said, 'That's mind blowing, boss, I don't know what to say to him'.

I would wait in silence for the men, these very rough and tough men, to ponder their answers. It usually took a little while before somebody spoke, and the requests they came up with were often very simple and always very down to earth and practical.

'I want a job when I get out'; 'I want my family back'; 'I want to start a new life free from crime'; and, much less frequently, 'I want to be pardoned'.

But of course, the question that Jesus asked of Bartimaeus is addressed in the end to every person, in or out of prison; and it is a question that he persistently asks. Only when we respond in deep honesty, and sometimes painfully, do we find, like Bartimaeus, our deepest needs are met.

Ron Dale

Proper 26/Ordinary Time 31
Fourth Sunday before Advent*

Sunday between 30 October and 5 November inclusive

Mark 12:28-34

*Love is . . .
love is what?*

Intuition

At the heart of the great commandment is a tired, overworked four-letter word. The word is *love*. I wonder what that word means to you? Love is . . . love is what?

Love is doing the washing up, whether it is our turn or not. Or does such behaviour simply teach others to be lazy and irresponsible?

Love is giving others whatever they ask. Or does such behaviour simply teach others to be spoilt and selfish?

Love is protecting others from harm and hurt. Or does such behaviour simply teach others to be careless and immature?

Love is always putting others first. Or does such behaviour simply undermine one's own true self-worth?

Love is preferring to give than to receive. Or does such behaviour simply deprive others of showing love to us?

Love is preferring to listen to the plaintive cries of others rather than to burden them with the deepest needs of our own souls. Or does such behaviour simply deprive us of the love we rightly need to receive?

Love is putting others first and ourselves last of all. Or does such behaviour simply inflate another's ego at the cost of our own?

At the heart of the great commandment is a tired, over-worked four-letter word. The word is *love*. I wonder what that word means to you? Love is . . . love is what?

*A reading for All Saints' Day will be found on page 203.

Thinking

Listen to Jesus' reply to the scribe and think through what Jesus is really trying to say. Do you hear one commandment, two commandments or perhaps even three commandments? And which of these commandments, I wonder, do you find most difficult to keep?

Perhaps there is just one commandment, and that commandment is to love. Listen to Jesus' reply to the scribe and think through what Jesus is really trying to say.

Or perhaps there are two rather different commandments. The first commandment is to love the Lord your God with all your heart, and with all your soul, and with all your mind, and with all your strength. The second commandment is to love your neighbour as yourself. Listen to Jesus' reply to the scribe and think through what Jesus is really trying to say.

Or perhaps there are really three rather different commandments. The first commandment is to love the Lord your God. The second commandment is to love your neighbour. The third commandment is to love yourself. Listen to Jesus' reply to the scribe and think through what Jesus is really trying to say.

Perhaps the first letter of John makes a very true and valid point when the author argues that those who do not love a brother (or a sister or a neighbour) whom they have seen, cannot love God whom they have not seen. In other words, love of neighbour becomes the prerequisite of the love of God.

Perhaps the commandment to love your neighbour as yourself is making the rather similar point that those who do not love themselves (whom they have the opportunity to know very well) cannot truly love the neighbour (whom they have the opportunity to know less well). In other words, love of self becomes the prerequisite of the love of neighbour.

Listen to Jesus' reply to the scribe and think through what Jesus is really trying to say. Do you hear one commandment, two commandments or perhaps even three commandments? And which of these commandments, I wonder, do you find most difficult to keep?

Leslie J. Francis
Personality Type and Scripture: Exploring Mark's Gospel

The Reverend S.J. Davies, the only survivor of the four military chaplains captured in Korea, in his book *In Spite of Dungeons*, records the Christian heroism and devotion in Father Emil Kapaun, a Roman Catholic chaplain of the American 1st Cavalry Division. Among the earlier prisoners of war who had known him before he died, his name had become a legend. Under the most desperate conditions, in the heart of winter, with temperatures below zero, when the prisoners were ill-nourished and ill-clad, many of them weak and ill, and some dying each day, he moved among the sufferers, inspiring them with his calm and selfless courage. Each night he made his rounds, praying with them 'in the wretched, lice-infested, unheated shacks'. His cheerfulness never failed, nor his sense of fun, for he took a mischievous pleasure in making surreptitious raids on the food supplies of their captors, invoking the prayers of Dismas, the Penitent Thief!

He endeared himself to men of all denominations and allowed no difference of creed to be a barrier in his ministry. And, says Padre Davies, he spent hours washing (without soap) the soiled underclothes of the sick and other prisoners. There was no limit to his Christian grace and love. He was only young. He died in captivity, worn out by dysentery and from a clot in his right leg. At a Protestant memorial service held for him in the camp, an American officer – a Baptist – recorded the details at the back of his tattered Bible, including the words of Major Joe Ryan, a British officer who conducted the service. 'He said that Father Kapaun certainly did not hide his light under a bushel, but the whole manner of his every-day life shone forth to the glory of our heavenly Father.'

Frederick C. Gill
The Glorious Company: Vol. 2

Emil J. Kapaun, a United States Army Chaplain, died in captivity in North Korea.

All Saints' Day, 1 November

John 11:32-44

I will tell you a Jewish story from the time soon after Christ. Some pagans were teasing a couple of little Jewish girls, and trying to laugh them out of their religion. What could be more absurd than the hope of resurrection? How shall the person rotted and gone to clay ever live and breathe again? The little Jewesses whispered together for a moment. Then one of them said: 'May I tell you a story, please?'

'Go on,' said the others.

'In our village,' said she, 'there were two potters. One of them could make pots out of water and clay. The other could make pots out of water alone. Which of them, do you think, was the more surprising in his skill?'

'Well, of course, you are talking nonsense,' they said, 'but if there were such men, the making of pots out of mere water would be much more surprising.'

'Then why are you more surprised,' said the child, 'that God should make new again out of clay, than that he should have made them out of a drop of water in the beginning?'

I don't think there is much to be added by the wisest head to this childish argument. If we believe in God at all, we believe in the Creator through whose will and power all things, including human beings, have come to be, not from a drop of water, but from nothing. If he makes us again, at least he has some materials; even though the way he works on them is an absolute mystery to us. Nevertheless, it would be a strange sort of belief which allowed God to have the power to create all things, and yet denied him the power to remake the human person.

The commemoration of All Saints is not concerned with those who lived particularly holy lives on earth, but with those whom the power of God has remade and brought through to heaven. To believe in the real existence of this great company is not to believe in something called the soul, which cannot die: it is to believe in God, and in his will to save us alive and bring us near himself. The saints have been made by God in their creation, and remade by him in their heavenly existence. But more, they have been made what they are by heavenly grace. God has not only given them existence, he has given them sanctity; and that is why we have fellowship with them, and are bound in one communion of saints. For the divine love which has triumphed in them will also conquer in us. If we want to know what God is doing with us, we look at these splendid beings who share the spontaneity of the Creator's mind, the delight of his heart and the breath of his love. Religion is not fundamentally a battle against sin, it is a drawing up together into glorification. God draws us above all through Jesus Christ, and Christ through all those who have gone before us, or who accompany us. Not all those, we think, who have left this earthly scene have yet reached that heavenly one, and so, as we rejoice in all saints today, we pray for all souls tomorrow, especially for the friends we knew, that God will join them to the saints, through Jesus Christ.

Austin Farrer
Words for Life

Proper 27/Ordinary Time 32
Third Sunday before Advent*

Sunday between 6 and 12 November inclusive

Mark 12:38-44

To give is at once expressive and liberating. To give up suggests reluctance.

During the building of Coventry Cathedral in the early 1960s I used to go over to Coventry from Birmingham where I was training for the Methodist ministry and observe how the cathedral was taking shape. And, because I happened to be at the right place at the right time, I was given a personal tour of the newly finished building.

I loved the space, the coloured windows that revealed the truth about God and humankind, the Bethlehem baptismal font, the tablets of the word and of course the huge tapestry of Christ in lovely green and gold.

Some weeks later I queued with my wife and two children to see the building again. As we were leaving, I noticed an offertory plate, a huge silver dish, by the exit. So I fished out some money for us all to give. As I was doing this, I saw a young scout in uniform standing by the plate. He was slowly turning out from his pockets an amazing variety of things: a piece of string, a battered hanky, some wire, one or two nails, until, right at the last, he found an old sixpence which he duly placed on the plate. It was all he had, and I remember being deeply moved by his gift. It put me in mind of the widow's mite, and I was delighted to know that the same spirit of generosity had not yet died out in this tired old world.

Ron Dale

It is a help to think of the life and death of Jesus as sacrifice, but the word needs to be used with care. In the world of religion a sacrifice is either an offering to the ultimately holy or the giving up of something in devotion to the holy. The two

*CWL Gospel is Mark 1:14-20. Appropriate readings will be found on page 56, Third Sunday of Epiphany.

ideas can blend in a single instance but it is wise to keep them apart because the first meaning is infinitely important, the second infinitely dangerous. To give is at once expressive and liberating. To give up suggests reluctance; it implies that one needs or is perhaps particularly identified by this thing which is to be surrendered for some laudable reason. There was nothing about Jesus that he wanted to keep. He found his identity in giving.

People who do not want to give think it is more blessed to give than to receive because giving is painful. There are others who actually sense the enjoyment of existence through giving, through spending and being spent. For these it is more blessed to give than to receive not because there is virtue in it but because there is happiness in it.

Jesus was this kind of giver. He is the great sign to us that life need not be dreary, need not be saved, but can be, must be, entirely spent. It is fear that makes us hold on to life or to what represents life's meaning for us. The cross marked the place in history where a superb victory over fear was won, the public fear in religion and politics, the private fear within the individual's insecurities. The proof of that is simply the verdict of time, that at the cross it is clear that life is represented by the man who died there and death by the people who put him there.

And he is still with us, after all these years, still making a huge difference to the life of the world.

Neville Ward
Five for Sorrow, Ten for Joy

Proper 28/Ordinary Time 33
Second Sunday before Advent

Sunday between 13 and 19 November inclusive

Mark 13:1-8

Apocalyptic literature speaks of what God is doing and will do both by means of and apart from historical events.

In 1774 another group of religious Utopians arrived in New York. It was tiny, consisting of a determined and charismatic leader, 'Mother' Ann Lee, and eight followers. They would receive the nickname of 'Shakers', from their shivering community dances that looked so odd to outside observers. They, however, called themselves the 'United Society of Believers in Christ's Second Appearing'. This miniature sect would ramify and increase over the next seventy-five years, only to go into a sharp decline by the end of the nineteenth century; but at the high tide of the movement, around 1850, there were probably 150,000 practising Shakers in America.

By the end of the 1780s, their first community near Albany had created missions, or 'families', in Connecticut and Massachusetts. Though Mother Ann died in 1784, the Shaker faith rode a wave of religious revivalism that followed the American Revolution. The northernmost Shaker community was founded in 1794, at Sabbathday Lake in Maine. Today, it is a museum unto itself – its meeting house and associated buildings still stand, but the community is down to eight people. Unlike the Quakers, they took no part in public life. They wished only to be left alone. They were self-sufficient. Most communities bought nothing from 'the world' except sugar, salt, molasses and raw metal.

Some Shakers were excellent craftsmen, and through the medium of their handiwork – mostly furniture – they came to influence American culture more strongly than any group of Utopian religious 'seekers' since the Puritans. Their effect, however, was delayed. Shaker aesthetic principles did not have much resonance outside the circle of the 'enlightened' until the twentieth century, when the purity and strict functional thought entailed in Shaker design was adopted, as ancestors often are in America, as precursor of modernist rationality. Why was it, over a long period during which 'mainstream' American design looked to Chippendale and Sheraton and moved gradually into the florid and often congested exuberance of the 1850s, that Shaker furniture kept its bareness to the eye, its foursquare beauty? The answer has to be sought in the Shakers' difference from other Americans – their religious beliefs.

Mother Ann Lee, the daughter of a Lancashire blacksmith, had been caught up in the great movement of working class religious 'enthusiasm' of mid-eighteenth century England. Like hundreds of thousands of others, she believed in direct revelation, not the rites and formality of the Anglican Church. Inspired by a vision, she believed the kingdom of God was not to be found in the official Church. It dwelled in each individual soul. The 'parousia' or Second Coming of Christ would not happen with public grandeur and clouds of glory; it was immanent within each believing man, woman and child. When the millennium came, which Ann Lee's followers expected it to do at any moment, it would be an internal event. But it required the right conditions: humility, community and remoteness from the 'worldly'.

The rules of Shakerism included a strictly observed equality of the sexes, and an equally strict celibacy. The sect could only expand by conversion. In the New Jerusalem there could be no mine and thine, no masters or servants. Every detail of life in the communities was enlaced by rules, the so-called Millennium Laws, which governed an infinity of matters from how to finish a workbench top to the correct way of climbing stairs in segregated order.

Once these conditions were met, the most ordinary life of work could fill with spiritual meaning, as the indwelling of Christ took hold. Hence the Shaker emphasis on the twin ideas of 'unity' and 'simplicity'. One fostered the other: unity, because the cohesion of the sect discouraged vanity and attachment to the world, fostered simplicity, the willing detachment from egotism and appetite that left the soul clear to be occupied by Christ. This applied to all aspects of Shaker life, and is implicit in their craftwork. 'Hands to work,' said a Shaker motto, 'and hearts to God.'

Robert Hughes
American Visions; The Epic History of Art in America

Mark 13:1-8 drops the reader down in terrain remarkably different from the biographical-type narrative of the remainder of the Gospel. Were the material not identified as Markan, one would guess it to be from Daniel or Revelation, for like those two books, Mark 13 is apocalyptic in nature. An apocalypse is an unveiling, a vision that grants its recipient a glimpse beyond what is going on to what is really going on. Half revealed, half concealed in language that is dramatic, filled with symbolic images and numbers, apocalyptic literature speaks of what God is doing and will do both by means of and apart from historical events. Scenes are painted on cosmic canvas, including heaven and earth, nature and human history, past, present and future. God's judging and redeeming activity will be so critical, so important, so final that to speak of it is to stretch and to burst the bounds of ordinary speech. It is a kind of religious literature embraced by persons in dire straits, who, seeing no relief from the sinful social, religious and political institutions, cling desperately to their faith and look to heaven for vindication.

. . . Jesus entered Jerusalem (Mark 11:1), went to the Temple, looked around and the next day (?) went again to the Temple, this time to cleanse it in an act that signalled the end of its function. Now in Mark 13:1, for the final time Jesus leaves the Temple and predicts its complete destruction. He is seated on the Mount of Olives opposite the Temple. Notice the language: Jesus is seated 'opposite' the Temple, the location itself being described in such a way as to alert the reader that what follows will be the end of the Temple system and the vindication of Jesus' life and work. Jesus is asked by the first four disciples whom he had called (verse 3) when this destruction would occur and what signs would announce it. In the discourse that follows, the end of the Temple, the end of all things, and the glorious coming of the Son of Man to gather his own (the Parousia) are interwoven themes. But perhaps clarity will be served by looking at the passage as a response to the two questions of the disciples: When? What signs?

. . . Jesus begins with a word of warning about false leaders and about misreading the signs of the end time. In desperate times desperate people will rally around those who seem to possess power and charisma. This is especially true if such would-be leaders invoke the name of Jesus and even say, 'I am' (verse 6), an expression sometimes used by Jesus that, by implication, associated him with God. . . . To be sure, Jesus shared the general view of Jewish apocalyptists that certain messianic woes would precede the end of history as it now is and the beginning of God's reign: convulsions in the natural world, violence in the social world. However, these crises are not the end but 'the beginning of the birth pangs' (verse 8). Something marvellous that God is doing is yet to arrive, to be born. In other words, keep your belief in the final act of

God, do not despair in these violent times, and do not be led by false teachers to abandon the mission. Be watchful and alert, to be sure, but endure in the task given to the Church: 'The Good News must first be proclaimed to all nations' (verse 10).

Fred B Craddock
Preaching Through the Christian Year: 'B'

Proper 29/Christ the King

Sunday between 20 and 26 November inclusive

John 18:33-37

Behold the Man!
(John 19:5)

Behold the Lamb!
(John 1:36)

Behold your King!
(John 19:14)

Behold your God!
(Isaiah 40:9)

The crown rights of Jesus

Here, in these four texts, we have a special pilgrim's progress of many a soul in its spiritual apprehension of the fact of Christ. *'Behold the Man!'* That, for many of us, is the first step to Christian faith: when we are gripped by the sheer manliness of Jesus. Then, in the soul's experience, that first step has led on to a second – *'Behold the Lamb of God!'* That has come next: they have been moved to the depths by the meaning of the sacrifice of Jesus. And then, these first and second steps together have led on to a third – *'Behold your King!'* That has been the third step: they have acknowledged the sovereign rights of Jesus. And then these three steps together have led on to a fourth – *'Behold your God!'* That has been the final step: they have the Man, the Lamb, the King, the God Incarnate – that has been the pilgrim's progress of many a soul in relation to the fact of Christ. It is the road that most young folk who are out-and-out for Christ today have travelled. It is the road that many who are just feeling their way in religion are travelling now – some of them quite slowly, held back by doubts and difficulties, and refusing (all honour to them for their refusal) to be hurried or stampeded into faith, or to take their religion at second hand. It is the road the first disciples went. And it is the road that the Church now exists to point out to pilgrim souls. Let us follow this road in thought.

Behold the Man!

Here, to begin with, was Pilate – proud, cold, haughty Roman; and on the balcony beside him this Jew from Nazareth, standing there with his hands bound with thongs, and the purple robe of mockery flung over his shoulders, and the blood from the crown of thorns streaming all over his face, and that mad mob in the street desperate to lynch him – 'Give us him, give us him! We'll rend and trample on him!' – and the prisoner, through it all, motionless, silent, with his eyes right up to God! And suddenly Pilate, flinging out his

211

right arm and pointing – 'Behold!' he cries, shouting above the clamour of the crowd, *'Behold the Man!'* Ah, Pilate, truer word you never spoke – *'the Man!'*

Reading recently in *Lawrence of Arabia* – that great and fascinating story – I came upon this sentence: 'No man,' it said, 'could lead the Arabs unless he ate the rank's food, wore their clothes, lived level with them, and yet appeared better in himself.' To that, I should like to add this: no one could lead the hosts of humanity unless he mingled with the rank and file, wore their human frame – bone of their bone, flesh of their flesh – living level with them all the time, and yet somehow beating them at their own game, beating them for sheer downright manliness! Isn't that the Christ?

'Behold the Man!' cried Pilate, and his words have come echoing down the centuries, have been taken up by soul after soul, have been cried aloud by the spirit of youth, catching sight of Jesus from afar, have swelled into a mighty volume of adoring praise – 'Behold the Man!' And that discovery is the first step to full faith in the Redeemer.

Behold the Lamb!

After that first stage of the road there comes a second. 'Behold the Lamb of God!' said John the Baptist. This is going deeper. This is more than manliness. This is sacrifice. This is suffering for others. This is love sweating blood. This is love confronting all the world's sorrow, shame and sin, and taking it upon itself. *'Behold the Lamb of God!'*

What is love? You can't define it. It has never by any poet or prophet or lover been defined. But if you ask me what is its central characteristic, I should say that it is *its readiness to take things upon itself.*

When Charles Dickens' fine old Yarmouth fisherman went out after his erring child in her shame, his Emily who had been the light of his life, went out searching for her, murmuring all the time, 'I'll go till I drop dead to find her' – what is it that you read on that drawn, haggard face? It is this – 'he is bearing her sin: he is *taking it upon himself.'*

When General Booth in his young days first felt the call of the slums, and the underworld and all life's pitiful wreckage; when he wrote describing his feelings then, 'I hungered for Hell, I pushed into the very midst of it, I loved it because of the souls I saw' – what do the gallant words mean but this – he was *taking it on himself.*

'Oh,' cried old John Duncan, thinking of the price Christ had to pay, 'oh, it was terrible, it was terrible, *it was damnation!* And – *he took it lovingly!'*

I think I can understand why it was that Denney, staunch rigid Protestant as he was, could yet declare, speaking one day to his students about the newer theology that was trying to construct a bloodless Gospel, and the newer theologians who were forgetting the cross, 'If I had to choose between being such a one, and being a Roman priest holding up a crucifix to the eyes of a dying man and saying "God loves like that," I had rather be the priest – every time.'

Yes, indeed! For what I see in the cross, and what you see in the cross, is not only someone summoning us to play the man in this hard, difficult world: it is someone caring enough for us to take everything on to himself, and to sink his very life in the cause of our happiness and peace. 'Behold the Man' – yes, manhood to perfection, manliness incarnate: but more, but deeper, but far more moving and subduing – Behold the sacrifice! Behold love's willing agony! 'Behold the Lamb of God!' It is the second stage on the road to full faith in the Redeemer.

Behold your King!

Now I am going to put this to you. If a person has taken the first step, and if they have then gone on and taken the second step, then they are bound in honour – sooner or later – to take the third step. If they have been fascinated by the sheer manliness of Jesus, and if they have been moved to the depths by the sacrifice of Jesus, then (if they are in earnest about this) they are bound to go on, and surrender to the sovereign rights of Jesus. 'Behold the Man!' 'Behold the Lamb of God!' What then? Add these two things together and they produce the most terrific challenge on this earth – *'Behold your King!'*

The writer to the Hebrews one day had a great vision, and he took up his pen and wrote the vision down. 'We see Jesus,' he wrote, 'crowned with glory and honour!' I am going to ask you – *do* we? 'We see Jesus crowned' – do we? If he were really crowned in the heart and affection of the world, would there be any war? Would there be any slums? Would there be any running after salacious plays and films and novels? 'We see Jesus crowned' – look into your own heart, and then tell God: is it *true?*

. . . And you know that whatever your difficulties about

religion may be; whatever your criticisms (many of them perfectly justified, I know) about us blundering folk who profess Christ in this world, and misrepresent him; whatever your dislike of the slow, sometimes painfully slow, machinery of the Church that bears his name, and of its delays in giving his will effect – whatever your feelings on all these matters may be, here is one challenge that none of these things touches, one challenge that remains and will remain through everything: *What about Christ and your own life?* Has he yet got the throne? Are you prepared to take the final step, the step of a soul's bounden honour? 'Behold the Man! Behold the Lamb of God! And therefore, soul of mine, *behold your King!'*

Have we vision enough to see that whatever conscience and Christ may cost us, whatever the shrinking of our hearts from full surrender, this settles it – he has a claim on you. By his perfect manhood, by his sacrificial suffering, he has a claim on you. Behold the Man! Behold the Lamb of God! And therefore (soul of mine – stand to attention!) *behold your King!*

Last of all and most of all – 'Behold your God!'

What is this Christianity I have been speaking of? It is not just loving your neighbour, or observing the Golden Rule, or living decently and respectably. It is the message that God has come right down into human life. God has broken through. God has acted. God has come.

God has come! God is here! At any moment, he may break through again. That is the world's hope. That is *'the* hope of every contrite heart, the joy of all the meek'. 'Behold the Man! Behold the Lamb! Behold your King! Behold your God!' Let him hear you say it now in the secret of your heart – 'O Jesus, forever I adore Thee! My Lord and my God!'

James S. Stewart
Walking with God

214

Index of Authors

Acknowledgements

The publishers wish to thank all those who have given their permission to reproduce copyright material in this publication. The readings listed below are all in copyright and the addresses of the copyright owners are given at the end of this section.

First Sunday of Advent

God comes . . . (Ira E. Williams), taken from *God in Unexpected Places*, published by Abingdon Press, 1974. Used by permission.

Come, Lord Jesus . . . (Ira E. Williams), taken from *God in Unexpected Places*, published by Abingdon Press, 19xx. Used by permission.

What is the significance . . . (Lamar Williamson, Jun.), taken from *Mark (Interpretation Series)*, published by Westminster John Knox Press, USA. Used by permission.

Second Sunday of Advent

In Paul's letter . . . (John Timmer), © Copyright Control.

The chief actor . . . (John V. Taylor), taken from *The Go-between God*, SCM Press 1972. World rights outside US. Used by permission.

Why Jesus never wrote a book . . . (Ron Dale), © Ron Dale.

Third Sunday of Advent

Ain't it wonderful . . . (Fynn), taken from *Mister God, This is Anna*, published by Harper-Collins Publishers Ltd. Used by permission.

If Christ is not the light . . . (A. E. Whitham), © Copyright Control.

Fourth Sunday of Advent

Advent used to be known . . . (Denys Thompson), taken from *Readings*, published by Cambridge University Press, 1974. Used by permission.

Not long ago . . . (Penelope Duckworth), taken from *Teaching Sermons on the Incarnation*, published by Abingdon Press, 1998.

Christmas Day – First Proper

The Shepherd's Carol (Anon), © Copyright Control.

Blake among angels . . . (Peter Ackroyd), taken from *Blake*, published by Sinclair-Stevenson. Used by permission of Random House UK Ltd.

When Christ was born . . . (Ira E. Williams), taken from *God in Unexpected Places*, published by Abingdon Press, 1974. Used by permission.

On Saturday I told him . . . (J. B. Priestley), taken from *Lost Empires*, published by Heinemann. Used by permission of Peters Fraser and Dunlop Group Ltd.

Christmas Day – Second Proper

Over the last twenty . . . (Ron Dale), © Ron Dale.

My predecessor . . . (Eric James), taken from *Judge Not: A Selection of Sermons*, published by Christian Action, and used by permission of the author.

They knelt at the manger . . . (Ira E. Williams), taken from *God in Unexpected Places*, published by Abingdon Press, 1974. Used by permission.

Christmas Day – Third Proper

Back to basics . . . (Colin Morris). Used by permission of the author.

First Sunday of Christmas

So it's not only tender . . . (Eric James), taken from *Judge Not: A Selection of Sermons*, published by Christian Action, and used by permission of the author.

When the Rubic Cube . . . (Ron Dale), © Ron Dale.

Towards the end . . . (David Mowbray), © David Mowbray. Used by permission of Jubilate Hymns.

It is a wonderful thing . . . (William Barclay), taken from *Daily Study Bible: The Gospel of Luke*, published by The Saint Andrew Press, 1994. Used by permission.

The birth of Jesus . . . (Beverly R. Gaventa), taken from *Texts for Preaching – Year C* by Charles B. Cougar, Beverly R. Gaventa, J. Clinton McCann and James D. Newsome, © 1994 Westminster John Knox Press, USA. Used by permission.

Second Sunday of Christmas

Enough, said God . . . (Ted Hughes), taken from *What is the Truth?*, published by Faber and Faber Ltd. Used by permission.

Necessary elements . . . (T. D. Meadley), taken from *Top Level Talks*, © 1969 Epworth Press. Used by permission of Methodist Publishing House.

Harry Lime . . . (Graham Greene), taken from *The Third Man*, published by Penguin. Used by permission of David Higham Associates Ltd.

Planet earth . . . (Sarah Sarkhel), taken from *Liturgy of Life*, edited by Donald Hilton. Used by permission of the National Christian Education Council.

On Sunday, January 31st . . . (Andrew Chaikin), taken from *A Man on the Moon*, published by Penguin Books Ltd. UK and British Commonwealth, excluding USA. Used by permission.

Over the last twenty years . . . (Ron Dale), © Ron Dale.

The Epiphany

The journey of the Magi . . . (Eric James), taken from *Judge Not: A Selection of Sermons*, published by Christian Action, and used by permission of the author.

When we told him . . . (Michel Tournier), taken from *Gaspard, Melchior et Balthazar*. Used by permission of Editions Gallimard, Paris.

The Baptism of the Lord

From time to time . . . (Eric James), taken from *Judge Not: A Selection of Sermons*, published by Christian Action, and used by permission of the author.

Second Sunday of Epiphany

The biblical word . . . (Fred B. Craddock), taken from *Preaching Through the Christian Year B: A Comprehensive Commentary on the Lectionary*, © Fred B. Craddock, John H. Hayes, Carl R. Holladay and Gene M. Tucker. Used by permission of Trinity Press International, USA.

After spending an exhilarating . . . (Ron Dale), © Ron Dale.

Third Sunday of Epiphany

Intuition. The central theme . . . (Leslie J. Francis), taken from *Personality, Type and Scripture*, published by Cassell plc. Used by permission.

Thinking. The key question . . . (Leslie J. Francis), taken from *Personality, Type and Scripture*, published by Cassell plc. Used by permission.

Humour, wonder and the other . . . (Walter J. Burghardt, SJ), taken from *Grace on Crutches: Homilies for Fellow Travellers*, © 1986 Walter J. Burghardt, SJ. Used by permission of Paulist Press Inc., USA.

Fourth Sunday of Epiphany

Jesus did not live up to his teaching . . . (J. Middleton Murray), taken from *The Life of Jesus*, © Copyright Control.

Because I got very tired . . . (Ron Dale), © Ron Dale.

Jesus leads people . . . (Hugh Martin), taken from *The Parables of the Gospels*, SCM Press 1937. World rights. Used by permission.

Fifth Sunday of Epiphany/Proper 1

Hollywood film star . . . (Loretta Young), © Copyright Control.

Feeling. Here is a tale . . . (Leslie J. Francis), taken from *Personality, Type and Scripture*, published by Cassell plc. Used by permission.

Sixth Sunday of Epiphany/Proper 2

Intuition. In the ancient . . . (Leslie J. Francis), taken from *Personality, Type and Scripture*, published by Cassell plc. Used by permission.

Feeling. Awake from slumber . . . (Leslie J. Francis), taken from *Personality, Type and Scripture*, published by Cassell plc. Used by permission.

Seventh Sunday of Epiphany/Proper 3

Forgive no more . . . (L. Gregory Jones), taken from *Embodying Forgiveness: A Theological Analysis*, © 1995 Wm. B. Eerdmans Publishing Co. Used by permission.

Eighth Sunday of Epiphany/Second Sunday before Lent

I was to be fifty . . . (H. A. Williams), taken from *Some Day I'll Find You*, published by Mitchell Beazley (a division of Octopus Publishing Group Ltd). Used by permission.

What can a person say . . . (Ernest T. Campbell), © Copyright Control.

Ninth Sunday of Epiphany

Intuition. The Pharisees were . . . (Leslie J. Francis), taken from *Personality, Type and Scripture*, published by Cassell plc. Used by permission.

Feeling. Now see how the . . . (Leslie J. Francis), taken from *Personality, Type and Scripture*, published by Cassell plc. Used by permission.

Last Sunday after Epiphany/Sunday next before Lent

Sensing. The transfiguration . . . (Leslie J. Francis), taken from *Personality, Type and Scripture*, published by Cassell plc. Used by permission.

Intuition. Just occasionally . . . (Leslie J. Francis), taken from *Personality, Type and Scripture*, published by Cassell plc. Used by permission.

Thinking. If we are going . . . (Leslie J. Francis), taken from *Personality, Type and Scripture*, published by Cassell plc. Used by permission.

Sight, light, illumination . . . (Austin Farrer), taken from *Words for Life*. Used by permission of the Trustees of the late Mrs Katherine Farrer (BKL Weeks Green).

First Sunday of Lent

I sat in the desert . . . (Barbara Brown Taylor), taken from *Bread of Angels*, © 1997 Barbara Brown Taylor, published by Cowley Publications, USA, and distributed in the UK by Columba Book Service, Dublin. Used by permission.

Second Sunday of Lent

The scandal . . . (Tom Meadley). Used by permission of Mrs Joan Meadley.

Among the Jews . . . (Hans-Ruedi Weber), taken from *On a Friday Noon* (p. 70), © 1979 World Council of Churches, Geneva. Translated from Cyril, in Migne, in *Patrologia Graeca 33*, 805 B. Used by permission.

Third Sunday of Lent

Two summers ago . . . (Barbara Brown Taylor), taken from *The Preaching Life*, © 1993 Barbara Brown Taylor, published by Cowley Publications, USA, and distributed in the UK by Columba Book Service, Dublin. Used by permission.

Fourth Sunday of Lent

Submission to the . . . (R. H. Strachan), taken from *The Fourth Gospel: Its Significance and Environment*, SCM Press 1917. World rights. Used by permission.

Billy Bathgate is the story . . . (E. L. Doctorrow), © Copyright Control.

Fifth Sunday of Lent

Here is a true story . . . (Frank G. Applegate), taken from *Indian Stories from the Pueblos*, © 1929 J. B. Lippincott. Used by permission of HarperCollins Publishers Inc., USA.

John 12:27 has Jesus . . . (John V. Taylor), taken from *The Go-between God*, SCM Press 1972. World rights outside US. Used by permission.

Palm/Passion Sunday

She has done a beautiful . . . (Lamar Williamson Jnr), taken from *Mark (Interpretation Series)*, published by Westminster John Knox Press, USA. Used by permission.

If ever I am disappointed . . . (Marie Curling).

Nina was captivated . . . (John Marshall), © Copyright Control.

When tanks rolled by . . . (David J. Harding). Used by permission of the author.

His master's voice . . . (Tom Meadley). Used by permission of Mrs Joan Meadley.

Easter Day

Prayer for Marilyn Monroe . . . (Ernesto Cardenal), taken from *Marilyn Monroe and other Poems*, published by Search Press Ltd. Used by permission.

Death is . . . (M. H. Duke), © Copyright Control.

Second Sunday of Easter

In the vocabulary of religion . . . (Harry E. Fosdick), taken from *What is Vital in Religion*, © 1955 Harper & Brothers, renewed © 1983 by Elinor F. Downs and Dorothy Fosdick. Used by permission of HarperCollins Publishers, Inc., USA.

Third Sunday of Easter

But hardly any artist . . . (Hans Kung), taken from *Credo*, SCM Press 1993. World rights. Used by permission.

In Luke's telling . . . (Fred B. Craddock), taken from *Preaching Through the Christian Year B: A Comprehensive Commentary on the Lectionary*, © Fred B. Craddock, John H. Hayes, Carl R. Holladay and Gene M. Tucker. Used by permission of Trinity Press International, USA.

Fourth Sunday of Easter

Dead Poets Society . . . (edited by Clive Marsh and Gaye Ortiz), taken from *Explorations in Theology and Films*, published by Blackwell Publishers Ltd. Used by permission.

This version of Psalm 23 . . . (Ron Dale), © Ron Dale.

Fifth Sunday of Easter

In the language of the prophets . . . (R. H. Strachan), taken from *The Fourth Gospel*, 3rd edition, SCM Press 1941. Used by permission of SCM Press Ltd.

Sixth Sunday of Easter

Coming in silence . . . (Edward Rothstein), © Copyright Control.

And joy is everywhere . . . (Rabindranath Tagore), © Copyright Control.

Seventh Sunday of Easter

At the onset . . . (Ernest Gordon), taken from *Miracle on the River Kwai*, published by HarperCollins Publishers Ltd. Used by permission.

Pentecost

There was something . . . (Ernest Gordon), taken from *Miracle on the River Kwai*, published by HarperCollins Publishers Ltd. Used by permission.

Shirley Valentine is a woman . . . (edited by Clive Marsh & Gaye Ortiz), taken from *Explorations in Theology and Films*, published by Blackwell Publishers Ltd. Used by permission.

Trinity Sunday

John records in this Gospel . . . (A. M. Hunter), taken from *Jesus Lord and Saviour*, SCM Press 1976. World rights. Used by permission.

Proper 4

Intuition. The Pharisees . . .

Feeling. Now see how . . . (Leslie J. Francis), taken from *Personality, Type and Scripture*, published by Cassell plc. Used by permission.

Proper 16

He who eats my flesh . . . (F. F. Bruce), taken from *The Hard Sayings of Jesus*, published by Hodder and Stoughton Ltd. Used by permission.

Where a messiah was . . . (Fred B. Craddock), taken from *Preaching Through the Christian Year B: A Comprehensive Commentary on the Lectionary*, © Fred B. Craddock, John H. Hayes, Carl R. Holladay and Gene M. Tucker. Used by permission of Trinity Press International, USA.

Whose table is it? (Anon.), © Copyright Control.

Proper 17

Not long ago . . . (Wilhelm Hauff), © Copyright Control.

Proper 18

Really there is no . . . (Leslie J. Francis), taken from *Personality, Type and Scripture*, published by Cassell plc. Used by permission.

The saying was . . . (F. F. Bruce), taken from *The Hard Sayings of Jesus*, published by Hodder and Stoughton Ltd. Used by permission.

Proper 19

This is one of the most . . . (William Barclay), taken from *Daily Study Bible: The Gospel of Luke*, published by The Saint Andrew Press, 1994. Used by permission.

This passage can only . . . (D. E. Nineham), taken from *Saint Mark: The Pelican Gospel Commentaries*, published by Penguin Books 1963. Used by permission.

Proper 20

Jesus took a little . . . (Leslie J. Francis), taken from *Personality, Type and Scripture*, published by Cassell plc. Used by permission.

In the centre . . . (Allan W. Eckert), taken from *The Frontiersman*, © 1967 Allan W. Eckert, © renewed 1995 by Allan W. Eckert. Used by permission of Little, Brown and Co., USA.

Proper 21

Saltless salt . . . (F. F. Bruce), taken from *The Hard Sayings of Jesus*, published by Hodder and Stoughton Ltd. Used by permission.

For or against . . . (F. F. Bruce), taken from *The Hard Sayings of Jesus*, published by Hodder and Stoughton Ltd. Used by permission.

Proper 22

You must thank – or blame . . . (Eric James), taken from *Judge Not: A Selection of Sermons*, published by Christian Action, and used by permission of the author.

At a late 19th century . . . (Flora Thompson), taken from *Still Glides the Stream*, published by Oxford University Press, 1984. Used by permission.

Man lives in the herd . . . (Bishop of Chelmsford), © Copyright Control.

Proper 23

Live dangerously . . . (Leslie J. Francis), taken from *Personality, Type and Scripture*, published by Cassell plc. Used by permission.

Gluttony at first sight . . . (Christopher Bryant), taken from *The Heart in Pilgrimage*, published by Darton, Longman and Todd Ltd, © 1980. Used by permission.

On our own . . . (Brother Roger of Taize), taken from *No Greater Love: Sources of Taize*, published by Geoffrey Chapman Mowbray, © Ateliers et Presses de Taize. Used by permission.

Proper 24

Edward Scissorhands . . . (edited by Clive Marsh and Gaye Ortiz), taken from *Explorations in Theology and Films*, published by Blackwell Publishers Ltd. Used by permission.

Between last Sunday's . . . (Fred B. Craddock), taken from *Preaching Through the Christian Year B: A Comprehensive Commentary on the Lectionary*, © Fred B. Craddock, John H. Hayes, Carl R. Holladay and Gene M. Tucker. Used by permission of Trinity Press International, USA.

Addresses of Copyright Owners

Abingdon Press, 201 Eighth Avenue South, Nashville, TN 37203, USA.

Ateliers et Presses de Taizé, F-71250, Taizé-Communauté, France.

Avon Books Inc., 1350 Avenue of the Americas, New York, NY 10019, USA.

A & C Black (Publishers) Ltd, Howard Road, Eaton Socon, Huntingdon, Cambs., PE19 3EZ.

Blackwell Publishers Ltd, 108 Cowley Road, Oxford, OX4 1JF.

Cambridge University Press, The Edinburgh Building, Shaftesbury Road, Cambridge, CB2 2RU.

Cassell Plc, Wellington House, 125 Strand, London, WC2R 0BB.

Cowley Publications, 28 Temple Place, Boston, Massachusetts 02111, USA. (Tel. 001-800-225-1534).

Darton Longman & Todd Ltd, 1 Spencer Court, 140-142 Wandsworth High Street, London, SW18 4JJ.

Edition Gallimard, 5 Rue Sebastien-Bottin, 75328 Paris Cedex 07, France.

Wm. B. Eerdmans Publishing Co., 255 Jefferson Avenue S.E., Grand Rapids, Michigan 49503, USA.

Faber and Faber Ltd, 3 Queen Square, London, WC1N 3AU.

Trustees of the Farrer Estate, BKL Weeks Green (Chartered Accountants), College Keep, 4-12 Terminus Terrace, Southampton, Hampshire, SO14 3QJ.

Forward Movement Publications, 412 Sycamore Street, Cincinnati, Ohio 45202-4195, USA.

The Rev. D.J. Harding, Peace-Care, 39 Halsdon Road, Exmouth, Devon, EX8 1SR.

HarperCollins Publishers Ltd, 77-85 Fulham Palace Road, Hammersmith, London, W6 8JB.

HarperCollins Publishers Inc., 10 East 53rd Street, New York, NY 10022-5299, USA.

The Harvill Press, Unit 2, Aztec Row, Berners Road, London, N1 0PW.

David Higham Associates Ltd, 5-8 Lower John Street, Golden Square, London, W1R 4HA.

Hodder and Stoughton Ltd, 338 Euston Road, London, NW1 3BH.

Canon Eric James, 11 Denny Crescent, London, SE11 4UY.

Jubilate Hymns, 4 Thorne Park Road, Chelston, Torquay, TQ2 6RX.

Little, Brown & Company, Time & Life Building, 1271 Avenue of the Americas, New York, NY 10020, USA.

Methodist Publishing House (Epworth Press), 20 Ivatt Way, Peterborough, PE3 7PG.

Mitchell Beazley (a division of Octopus Publishing Group Ltd), c/o Reed Books Library, Sanders Lodge Industrial Estate, Rushden, Northants., NN10 6RZ.

National Christian Education Council, 1020 Bristol Road, Selly Oak, Birmingham, B29 6LB.

Oxford University Press, Great Clarendon Street, Oxford, OX2 6DP.

Paulist Press, 997 Macarthur Blvd., Mahwah, NJ 07430, USA.

Penguin UK, 27 Wrights Lane, Kensington, London, W8 5TZ.

Peters Fraser & Dunlop, 503/4 The Chambers, Chelsea Harbour, London, SW10 0XF.

Random House UK Ltd. (Sinclair-Stevenson), 20 Vauxhall Bridge Road, London, SW1V 2SA.

SCM Press, 9-17 St Albans Place, London, N1 0NX.

Search Press Ltd, Wellwood, North Farm Road, Tunbridge Wells, Kent, TN2 3QR.

The St Andrew Press, 121 George Street, Edinburgh, EH2 4YN.

Trinity Press International, 4775 Linglestown Road, Harrisburg, PA 17112, USA.

Westminster John Knox Press, 100 Witherspoon Street, Louisville, KY 40202, USA.

World Council of Churches, 150 Route De Ferney, PO Box No. 2100, 1211 Geneva 2, Switzerland.